Pomegranate Garden

*A Selection of Poems
by Haydar Ergülen*

Haydar Ergülen

Haydar Ergülen was born in Eskişehir, Turkey, in 1956. He published his first political and cultural broadside paper, *Ekin* (Culture), with his friend Şahin Şencan, when they were in middle school. At the age of eighteen he wrote articles protesting the death by capital punishment of political activists Deniz Gezmiş, Hüseyin İnan and Yusuf Aslan, activities that led to his month-long confinement by the police and expulsion from high school. He later took a degree in Sociology from Middle Eastern Technical University and held the position of teaching assistant in the Communications Faculty of Eskişehir Anadolu University while pursuing a Master's Degree in marketing and public relations. In 1983 he moved to Istanbul and began writing advertising copy.

His first poems and short stories were published in 1972 in the Eskişehir magazine *Deneme* (Essay). In 1981 he placed second after the renowned poet Murathan Mungan in *Hürriyet Gösteri* magazine's poetry competition, and his poetry began to appear in such magazines as *Somut, Felsefe Dergisi, Türk Dili, Yusufçuk, Hürriyet Gösteri, Yarın, Yeni Biçem, Akatalpa, Sombahar, Nar, Yasak Meyve, Budala, Öküz, Hayvan, Ot, Bavul, Şiir-lik, Kitap-lık, Heves* and *Varlık*.

Ergülen's first book of poetry, *Karşılığını Bulamamış Sorular* (Questions Without Response), came out in 1981 and was followed in 1983 by his publication, along with poet-friends Adnan Özer and Tuğrul Tanyol, of *Üç Çiçek* (Three Flowers), which was recognised as the first magazine of Turkey's '1980s-Era Poets.' From 1986 onwards he contributed to the editorial board of *Şiir Atı* magazine, and went on to work with Eskişehir friends Rahmi Emeç and Erol Büyükmeriç on the editorial board of *Yazılıkaya Şiir Yaprağı*.

From 1998 to 2007 Ergülen wrote the column 'Open Letters' for the left-wing daily *Radikal* and contributed to the daily *BirGün*. From 2010 to 2012 he wrote regularly for *Cumhuriyet* newspaper. He continues to write for *BirGün's* Sunday supplement.

Ergülen is now serving as Director of the Izmir International Poetry Festival, the Eskişehir Tepebaşı International Poetry Festival, and the Nazım Hikmet International Poetry Event, organised by Ataşehir Municipality in Istanbul. He attends poetry festivals and translation workshops throughout Europe and leads creative writing workshops in Istanbul. For the last seven years Ergülen has taught Contemporary

Poetry at Boğaziçi University, lectured on poetry at Kadir Has and Bahçeşehir universities, and given public lectures each month in Eskişehir.

Ergülen continues to write poetry and short stories, and twenty-one books of his poetry, including two written especially for children, have been published in Turkey, while two collections of his work (*Carnet intime* and *Grenade ou Nar*, translated by Claire Lajus) have been published in France, with German, Italian and Bulgarian editions due to come out soon. In addition to these, numerous books of his criticism and essays, along with three anthologies that he edited, have been published since 2000.

Ergülen and his wife Idil have a daughter, Nar, and four cats. Gülten Akın, Özdemir İnce, Ece Ayhan, Ahmet Telli, Veysel Öngören, Metin Altıok, Enis Batur, Murathan Mungan, Salih Bolat and Ali Cengizkan are the poets he knew and liked in his years in Ankara. His favourite poets are Yunus Emre, Pir Sultan Abdal, Nazım Hikmet, Cemal Süreya, Ergin Günçe, and Federico Garcia Lorca. He also greatly admires the Anatolian folk singers Aşık Veysel, Aşık Mahzunî Şerif, and Neşet Ertaş.

Awards
1981 *Hürriyet Gösteri* magazine poetry prize (2nd) Unutulmuş Bir Yaz İçin
1996 Halil Kocagöz Poetry Prize – *Eskiden Terzi*
1997 Behçet Necatigil Poetry Prize – *40 Şiir ve Bir*
1997 Cahit Külebi Special Prize at Orhon Murat Arıburnu Awards – *40 Şiir ve Bir*
1998 Akdeniz Altın Portakal Poetry Prize – *40 Şiir ve Bir*
2005 Cemal Süreya Poetry Prize – *Keder Gibi Ödünç*
2008 Metin Altıok Poetry Prize – *Üzgün Kediler Gazeli*
2015 Honorary Prize of the Language Association (Dil Derneği)
2017 City of Mersin Prize for Literature

Mel Kenne is a poet who has translated much Turkish poetry and prose into English and who was a founding member of the Cunda International Workshop for Translators of Turkish Literature. He co-edited, with Saliha Paker, *What Have You Carried Over? Poems of 42 Days and Other Works by Gülten Akın* (Talisman House, Publishers, 2014), and, along with Saliha Paker and Amy Spangler, he edited *Aeolian Visions / Versions: Modern Classics and New Writing from Turkey* (Milet Publishing, 2013). He and Paker also co-translated Latife Tekin's novels *Dear Shameless Death* (*Sevgili Arsız Ölüm*) and *Swords of Ice* (*Buzdan Kılıçlar*), both published by Marion Boyers Publishers in 2000 and 2007 respectively. He has had six collections of poetry published, most recently *Take* (Muse-Pie Press, 2011) and a bilingual collection, *Galata'dan / The View from Galata*, translated by İpek Seyalıoğlu and published in 2010 by Yapı Kredi Publishers in Istanbul.

Saliha Paker is a retired professor of Translation Studies, Boğaziçi University, Istanbul, who continues to teach her PhD course in History of Translation in Ottoman and Modern Turkish Society. Also involved in translating modern Turkish poetry and fiction for thirty years, she ran the Cunda International Workshop for Translators of Turkish Literature (CIWTTL) from 2005 to 2016. She co-edited (with Mel Kenne and Amy Spangler) a book of translations produced by the Cunda Workshop, *Aeolian Visions / Versions. Modern Classics and New Writing from Turkey* (Milet Publishing 2013). Her English editions of Enis Batur's poetry in *Ash Divan* (2006) and Gülten Akın's in *What Have You Carried Over?* (2014, co-edited with Mel Kenne) were both published by Talisman House. More recently she served as an editor, with Mel Kenne and İdil Karacadağ, of *Turkish Poetry Today 2016*, published by Red Hand Books.

Caroline Stockford, a writer, poet, and translator from Abermawddach, Wales holds an MA in the History of the Turkish Language from SOAS, London University. She participated in the Cunda International Workshop for Translators of Turkish Literature from 2013 to 2015 and has translated Behçet Necatigil, Haydar Ergülen, Ferit Edgü, Lale Müldür, and küçük İskender into English, as well as several poems by Yunus Emre into Welsh. In addition, she has translated Dafydd ap Gwilym into Turkish and lectured at Goldsmith's College and in Istanbul and Eskişehir on Welsh-Turkish poetry translation. She participated in the Eskişehir International Poetry Festival, Radnor Fringe, the Stanza festival, and at events in Aberystwyth. Her poetry appeared in *Sharp as Lemons, Make time for Aberystwyth*, and *Into the Void*, online at 'I am not a silent poet' and 'Burning House Press,' and in Turkish in 'Gard Şiir Dergisi'. She has two sons and works at the International Press Institute in Vienna.

Pomegranate Garden

A Selection of Poems
by Haydar Ergülen

Edited by Mel Kenne,
Saliha Paker and Caroline Stockford

PARTHIAN

Parthian, Cardigan SA43 1ED www.parthianbooks.com
First published in 2019
© Haydar Ergülen 2019
© This translation by Mel Kenne, Saliha Paker and Caroline Stockford
ISBN 978-1-912681-42-6
Edited by Mel Kenne, Saliha Paker and Caroline Stockford
Cover Image: 'Pomegranates' by Ercüment Tarhan
Cover design by www.theundercard.co.uk
Typeset by Elaine Sharples
Printed and bound by 4edge Limited, UK
Published with the financial support of the Books Council of Wales
British Library Cataloguing in Publication Data
A cataloguing record for this book is available from the British Library.

This book is dedicated to the memory of Selhan Savcıgil-Endres (1957-2019), a valued member of the Cunda International Workshop for Translators of Turkish Literature

Contents

Love's Inflection in Turkish

You were silk, you'd taken a train from the east,
so they'd forget you were a small town in the past
you passed through your exile in a mantle of Turkish,
tongue-spun words aren't enough, you're finer than silk,
now so beautiful more Turkish than us all!

If I grew a verse in my mother's garden, she would comprehend
the pitiless child in my tongue: even if I said,
'D'you think the rose would mind if the tulip were picked instead?'
not my rosemother, she'd remain a rose,
in Turkish no ugly flower grows!

You know my friend the sea
received a petition from the people's provinces
misspelled but signed by many hands,
requesting that love's case be drawn up forthwith,
Turkish drew love's inflection from the sea!

Would there be Turkish if it weren't for love?
I said, it's made from Turkish what you call wine
—since the grape-eyed sea's just useless—
I said, what would that poet fellow eat, drink, write
if he didn't steal the cherry from the garden of Turkish!

Hafız

Translated by Saliha Paker and Mel Kenne
from Hafız and Salamander (2002)

Foreword

This first selection of Haydar Ergülen's poetry to be presented to the English-speaking public is composed of poems picked out by the poet himself from his earliest collection in 1982 to his most recent one in 2019, and it includes a wide range of lyrical, narrative, and epigrammatic works. Ergülen is considered a leading figure of the 1980s generation of Turkish poets, one who is among the most representative of its poetic characteristics[1], while holding fast to his unique aspirations. We hope, therefore, that readers will emerge from this book with a clear view of how his poetry has evolved and an appreciation of why it has remained fresh over the years, maintaining its hold over its Turkish followers, young and old alike, since the early 1980s.

Haydar Ergülen's poetry unquestionably draws upon and expresses many of the basic forces that continue to shape Turkish culture and literature; however, its central focus is the common, down-to-earth concerns of humanity itself. At the core of Ergülen's work is the pervasive sense of poetry-writing as an inseparable part of life: that the co-existence of poetry, goodness and love is indispensable to the poet as a human being.

Approximately a third of the poems in our selection were translated at two workshops[2] held in 2006 and in 2013, while the rest of the translations were carried out in preparation for this book in consultation with the original team of translators. Ergülen was invited to participate as guest poet to both of the workshops. In a talk at the first workshop in 2006, Ergülen defined his poetry as one of *nasip*, his 'lot in life':

> A poet should write with few words and, if possible repeat a word more than once. 'Oh fall to my share,' he should implore, and should believe that each word

---

[1] Baki Asiltürk, *Türk Şiirinde 1980 Kuşağı*, Istanbul, Yapı Kredi Yayınları, 2011. 147.

[2] The Cunda International Workshop for Translators of Turkish Literature (CIWTTL, Türk Edebiyatı Çevirmenleri Cunda Uluslararası Atölyesi, TEÇCA (tecca.boun.edu.tr), which ran from 2006 to 2016, was supported by Boğaziçi University, Department of Translation and Interpreting Studies, and funded by the Turkish Ministry of Culture and Tourism.

is indeed his lot, so he should leave other words for someone else, for others too to have their share of words...

I believe in *nasip* even as I 'aspire' to write poetry. Each poem, and each poet even, has her or his lot, or share, of words. That is why, even if I do not regard them as my own 'property,' I think that certain words are/have become special to certain poets. And that is why I believe that a poet should write with few words. I look for these words in the works a poet has written (or even in the ones he has not written). In this way, I think, the poet would have to keep his grasp on his own issues, avoid wasting the accumulated vocabulary of another poet, and be 'satisfied with his own lot.' [3]

Acceptance in humility appears as an essential element in Ergülen's poetics, as does the very aspiration or desire (*heves*) to write poetry. Referring to 'Mother' (p. 10), the first poem in his earliest collection (*Questions Without Response*, 1982), which he wrote in memory of his friends who were killed following the military coup of September 12th, 1980, he says:

(This poem) aspires to raise a silent objection, if not resistance, to the inhuman practices of those days. 'Mother' is one of my most popular poems among readers, critics and poets. It can also be considered a summary of my poetry. As some critics have rightfully argued, the sound of my poetry has not changed much since those days and that particular poem. I can even maintain that it has not changed at all. The words and images I used have not changed much either: 'mother,' 'child,' 'pain,' 'bird,' 'rain' ... Throughout the years I added new words and images to these, but the new ones have not been that new, different, or as colourful. In a way, they are all colours that have a place in the same picture, images that can be thought of in the same framework. Here are some of the words and themes: 'goodness,' 'grief,' 'love,' 'home,' 'brotherhood/sisterhood,' 'nature,' 'countryside,' 'balcony,' 'courtyard,' 'garden,' 'aspiration,' 'word,' 'letter,' 'friendship,' 'death,' 'body,' 'paper,' 'memories,' and 'poetry.'[4]

---

[3] From Haydar Ergülen's talk in 2006 at the CIWTTL, partly translated by Şehnaz Tahir Gürçağlar for *Aeolian Visions / Versions: Modern Classics and New Writing from Turkey*. Eds. Mel Kenne, Saliha Paker, Amy Spangler. Milet Publishing, UK. 2013. 63-64.

[4] Ibid.

In due course, other themes emerge in his poetry, such as 'pomegranate,' 'sea,' and 'provinces.' 'Pomegranate' (p. 19), *Nar* in Turkish, makes its appearance in *40 Şiir ve Bir* (*40 Poems and One*), which he began to compose in 1996 and which would win him three prestigious awards in 1997 and1998: the Behçet Necatigil Prize for Poetry, the Antalya Golden Orange Prize, and the Cahit Külebi Special Prize. A chapbook published concurrently carries the 'summary of the first 42 years of his life in poetry':

> I was born on October 14, 1956 in Eskişehir as the first child of Nazlıgül and Hasan. My father was an auto mechanic, my mother a housewife. I had five more brothers and sisters. As a family, we were all kids, we all remained kids. I had my first schooling in Eskişehir, then went to high school in Ankara, where I also got my degree in Sociology from Middle East Technical University... I began writing short stories, about twenty of which were published in 1971-73, when I was still in high school and during my first years at university. My first poem came out under a pseudonym in a magazine in 1973. When I lost my closest friend Şahin ('Lost Brother', p. 30) in a railway accident, I went back to writing poetry, and that was it. My maternal grandfather, Hüseyin Efendi, was also a poet. He composed folk songs and sang them to his stringed instrument, the saz. I could neither sing nor play, I just wrote...'. [5]

By 1998 Haydar Ergülen had already published five collections, having also assumed in the meantime two different authorial personae, evidently under Pessoa's influence[6]. One is Lina Salamandre in a fascinating book composed of songs and letters presumably by Lina, a character 'born of fire' – Haydar Ergülen's own invention – who gives voice to her passionate but unhappy relationship with Ruth Huntley ('No One's Closer to Me than Your Remoteness', p. 13).

Ergülen's other persona, Hafız, the poet, is a completely different character whose name instantly recalls the classic 14th century Persian Sufi poet, Hafız of Shiraz. In his biographical summary, Ergülen mentions Hafız simply as 'a fellow whose poetry has been coming out in magazines for the past three years. He will soon be free of me in 1999 with a book of his own.'[7] This book turns out to be *Hafıza* (Memory). 'Love's

---

[5] Haydar Ergülen (40 Şiir ve Bir). Short autobiography in *Andaç 1998*. Antalya: Altın Portakal Kültür ve Sanat Vakfı.

[6] Haydar Ergülen, Preface to *Hafız ile Semender*. Toplu Şiirler 2. Istanbul, Adam. 2002. p.15

[7] Haydar Ergülen (40 Şiir ve Bir). Short autobiography in *Andaç 1998*. Antalya: Altın Portakal Kültür ve Sanat Vakfı.

Inflection in Turkish' (p. xii), which appropriately resonates with the origins and early tradition of Turkish poetry, is from this collection.

We may claim that more recently Ergülen has assumed a third persona, that of *abdal*: the traditional epithet given to wandering mystics or dervishes of Alevi belief, who sang their poetry to the accompaniment of their music. Here is how Ergülen contrasts their self-effacement with the glaring visibility of the poets of our day:

> Once men went about delivering poetry yet remained unseen
> they were the dervish, the abdal, the poet, dervish lost
> abdal epithet, poet solitary, a bundle full of words, a chest full of spirit
> they are no more, of no use, now is the time of the fierce dervish, trendy abdal,
> fresh shaman poet. With no single aspiration, with
> not a thought for his lot, among the people yet against them
> in shallow waters seeking depth in meaning, in royalty's longboat
> yet adrift with the others, he wishes to be seen not
> as the oarsman but as the dervish by all and sundry.
> Now poethood is visible. The poets have come into plain sight.[8]

Ergülen's hereditary roots and his early family grounding in the Alevî abdal tradition, find full expression in a recent long narrative poem, 'Abdal Going Slowly on His Way' (p. 100), which is included in our selection. Here the poet is shown to be on a spiritual and artistic journey, continuing the tradition in the path of his 'sovereign,' Hacı Bektaş Velî[9]:

> He's my sovereign and comrade, my ongoingness
> lifeless walls he rides driving them on and on
> in a pigeon's habit he flies, in a gazelle's races onward
> in a lion's company has crossed this town often
> it's abdal who now slowly spreads
> Hacı Bektaş Velî's paths
> with the poems of his ongoingness:

---

[8] From Haydar Ergülen's talk (2006, CIWTTL), translated by Saliha Paker for this book.

[9] Hacı Bektaş Veli (1281-1338), a saintly Sufi figure, legendary for his miracles, who is honoured by Alevî-Bektaşî socio-religious communities.

4

Ergülen rules over this poem as Abdal, casting his own 'modern' vision into the mysteries and rituals of the Alevî bardic tradition, or 'ongoingness', as he puts it. Especially significant is the concept of 'the Mother' and various manifestations of femaleness not only in nature, but in human-made objects like 'courtyard' and 'woodwork,' as well as in thought and emotion, and in life experience, all of which celebrate creativity in the poem:

> One born bears life, the tree bears life, and the courtyard
> because all things start out female
> feelings, images, poems, words
> the leaf's female, water's female, the apple's female
> sleep's female, while dreams, I'd say, are angels,
> I can't vouch for the traveller, but the journey's female

Ergülen believes that 'a poem should have a mystery to it beyond a string of fine and meaningful words... I don't know if the mystery involves a quest for truth, or if it involves being satisfied by some lack while achieving completion, or simply by leaving something out...'[10]

The sense of mystery In 'Abdal Going Slowly On His Way' permeates the whole poem, which concludes with the enigmatic lines: 'between two eyebrows a mother has her seat / this poem doesn't end here it's only complete.' In this narrative of a journey the reader can perceive the unique merging of Haydar Ergülen's poetics and ethics.

Equally significant is Ergülen's earlier poem 'Pomegranate,' in *40 Poems and One* (1997), generally considered his poems of maturity, which he began to write the year before, when, as he puts it, 'I married İdil. With her I opened out to 40 poems — out of the rooms onto the streets...'[11]. In an interview given in the same year, Ergülen states that he spent his childhood 'more like an adult than a child, mostly reading books.' So when he grew older he 'fell in pursuit of his childhood, looking for it as his lost garden.' Ergülen continues: 'the dreams I had in my forties were very different from those in my twenties. Excess of words, 'being literary,' seeking depth in youthful

---

[10] Haydar Ergülen (40 Şiir ve Bir). Short autobiography in *Andaç 1998*. Antalya: Altın Portakal Kültür ve Sanat Vakfı.

[11] Ibid.

angst, all that was gone, instead poetry became one of the most natural states of mind for me in trying to understand the world and humanity. Mature poetry seemed to arrive with clarity and precision.'[12]

'Pomegranate,' like 'Abdal Going Slowly on His Way,' holds a special place in Ergülen's corpus of poetry. It is the only full poem about this fruit that reoccurs as the poet's favourite among other fruits that appear in his poems, including the cherry, the apple and the olive. Here we see the full flowering of the pomegranate as a complex metaphor for home, garden and neighbours, living and sharing in fellowship. The metaphor expands, embracing the language of poetry as well as love, offering a poetic refuge not only from a winter of darkness but also from the 'rough hand' that could also destroy the 'garden within garden' of love and the poetry of 'a thousand and one warm words of summer.' Perhaps what 'Pomegranate' best signifies is Ergülen's ethics of an ideal *iyilik*, which can best be translated as 'goodness' that also involves 'healing,' a state of mind celebrated more and more frequently in his recent poems.

'Writing poetry is a form of goodness,' runs a line in one of these poems ('Form', p. 76). 'Poetry of Goodness' is how Coşkun Yerli defines Ergülen's work that 'seems to convey the good-natured quality of a Turkmen dervish.'[13] Another fellow poet describes him as 'Working in the Store of Goodness,' while yet another suggests that in *40 Poems and One*, goodness dwells in peace with love, and the pomegranate is their home.[14]

In 'Pomegranate' an essential point of reference is, again, Ergülen's attachment to the Alevî-Bektaşî [15] tradition, which holds this fruit as a symbol of harmonious unity in plurality. Yet further telling references appear in such lines as 'let's head for the pomegranate.' These echo the famous refrain of the ballad, 'Let the Gates Open, Let's Head for the Shah,' by Pir Sultan Abdal [16], the legendary 16th century Alevî bard,

---

[12] Baki Asiltürk, *Türk Şiirinde 1980 Kuşağı*, Istanbul, Yapı Kredi Yayınları, 2011. 139-140.

[13] Coşkun Yerli, 'İyiliğin Şiiri,' in *40 Şiir ve Bir Odağında Haydar Ergülen Şiiri*. Antalya: Altın Portakal Kültür ve Sanat Vakfı, 1998. 63,68.

[14] Sina Akyol, 'İyilik Dükkanında Çalışıyor Haydar Ergülen,' in Haydar Ergülen (40 Şiir ve Bir). *Andaç 1998*. Antalya: Altın Portakal Kültür ve Sanat Vakfı.

[15] V. Bahadır Bayrıl, 'Beyaza İltica Eden bir Şiirin Ana Aksları,' in *40 Şiir ve Bir Odağında Haydar Ergülen Şiiri*. Antalya: Altın Portakal Kültür ve Sanat Vakfı, 1998. 17-20.

[16] Haluk Öner, 'Haydar Ergülen'in Şiirinde Alevî-Bektaşî Geleneğinin İzleri.' Unpublished essay.

who called out to his people to seek refuge with the Shah of Persia and join forces against the oppressive Ottoman governor in the East. Similarly, in the same poem, 'If a rough hand enters the pomegranate's garden' harks back to another well-known refrain by Pir Sultan Abdal: 'A Rough Hand has Entered our Friend's Garden', bringing destruction to his community. 'Pomegranate' is more than a poem about a fruit; it is a passionate warning against the deprivation of human values.

As readers will no doubt notice, Ergülen's invocations and personal interpretations of tradition, which go back to classical Ottoman language and poetry ('Translation', p. 54), in no way confine the thematic richness of his poems but contribute to their diversity. Ergülen's excellent command over the history of Turkish poetry, past and present, makes him a poet of poets, a believer in the fellowship of poets. This is revealed by allusions and explicit references to such leading figures as Cemal Süreya, Edip Cansever, Turgut Uyar and Ece Ayhan of the Second New Movement of the 1970s, but also to Atilla İlhan and Sezai Karakoç, from the older generation and to Seyhan Erözçelik, his contemporary, all of whom show up in this volume. Cemal Süreya is probably Ergülen's favourite, the figure to whom he pays special tribute in 'We're Lonely, Brother Cemal' (p. 25), and in his long, playful, autobiographical narrative, 'On Things That Are Falling Asleep' (p. 56).

As editors as well as participating translators, we have focused on offering readers the widest selection of Haydar Ergülen's poetry possible in a volume of this size. Moreover, we have done our best to retain the richness of nuance and depth of meaning that characterise most of the work presented in these pages. For we believe that Haydar Ergülen deserves not only to be recognised as an original poet who has earned a position of distinction in his own country, but that his work proves him worthy of being ranked among the major writers in the world today.

— Saliha Paker

I.

Mother

was I truly born of you mother
as roads, rivers, early noon stood by
would a child be born of a human

if your heart were made of stone, mother, could it still endure
if it were a bird or a flower or daylight
wouldn't a sprig of violet snap at the stem in pain

let the mountains give birth to me this time mother
and you be the warm rain
falling ceaselessly on my bleeding wounds

Translated by Saliha Paker and Mel Kenne
from Questions Without Response (1982)

My Neck, a Waste Land

I have no water oh night angel how I thirst
— hush writer the stream runs inside you
unsated by drinking more than your heart's fill

I have no voice oh almighty how I long to speak
— oh mute one who choked off his words
you went quiet, turned the earth into a wasteland

I have no light oh keeper of the void how my eyes hurt
— blind one unable to see his own candle
you became a moth to inwardly-burning flames

I have no body oh my moon-maker woman I go to you
— forget the banned lovemaking that revives you
the reason your flesh wants for water

I have no poetry oh fine letter to set in my notebook
— take off boy go into exile in the heart's land
they've broken their pen on your neck

Translated by Saliha Paker and Mel Kenne
from Poems of the Bridge to Hell (1991)

The Cape

I'm hiding your face, don't you fall,
not ever again, little waltzing smile,
as I tarry getting to a girl left in play
with every mother I relive the farewell

you have won over love, little girl
but love can never fill up this beauty

taking no time for the cliff edge, you walked away
taking no time to search, you went off to find
the cape that slipped off your childhood's sleep

the little girl passenger of balconies
the address of the dreamer, not those living the dreams
it's why getting used to an open wound
is like nurturing a rose that opens for no one

a suicide newly arisen from love is motherless
each one shuns the other, visits are made
and the balcony pulls no one into its beauty

for a sighing dream is too old to die
with memories on autumn balconies

you've overcome love little girl and your beauty
was daring enough to win a farewell

*Translated by Mel Kenne and Saliha Paker
from* The Street Princess (1990)

No One's Closer to Me than Your Remoteness!

It's the robbers, Ruth, I'm so afraid of them
they'll hunt me down like an apple soon
the wind will soon whisk me away to other gardens
the hunters are already in sight
so is the world, Ruth, all besides you

besides this forest, besides myself
your faroffness is the one place I can go
give me your tongue, Ruth, shield me with your distance
no one's closer to me than your remoteness!

Translated by Mel Kenne and Saliha Paker
from A 'Sister' Retired from the Cabaret (Lina Salamandre) (1990)

Once a Tailor

wear me out, make a tailor
of what's left of me, so there is no
try-on! the aching and hurting skin
makes the body undo the stitches

I was a tailor once, in meagre times
I had a shop, my first shirt
flew from my skin too soon, such desire
now foreign to my heart

cut me out some rain from your skin
right where we grew apart, those scissors
left the memory rusty! underground
the button, no skin but solitude

desire's now oversized

Translated by Şehnaz Tahir Gürçağlar
from Once a Tailor (1995)

Kuzguncuk Hotel

I cheated on my home for a street, over me
a moon in this town's silver quarter street
I'm the third floor up, the sea looks at me
from now on I'm just facing the sea

hey lay off me moon lady, at this Kuzguncuk hotel
go up to a virtuous floor, to your weighty guests
I'm only a life spent waiting on a memory

this is my soul's very first hotel stay
in the same room, same bed, same mirror
for the first time we see each other, no more goodbyes
I have to sleep with a stranger lying over me

don't set sail from this soul's quarter moon lady
I'm not ready for you, I'm on your side
whoever moves in I can't leave my home inside

this Kuzguncuk hotel of such many-storied goodness
like stars soaring ever upwards hey moon lady,
this child from some place you remember
this child from some place I have to forget

Translated by Mel Kenne
from Once a Tailor (1995)

15

Borrowed Dagger

how you bear this dagger
that way, whose back you took it from
and your skill in passing from
one blade edge to the other

I see a dual otherness in you
one sharp and orphaned
the other proud and silken

it's not as if you're bearing the dagger
so much as the dagger's borne on your back
the whites still seeping into your blood
you'll have to consult with the dagger
about the silk

yet the whites stay so distant
from a kiss with a blade between the teeth
see, nobody's knife stays with someone else,
my blood runs cold, building up rust
upon rust not even silk
waits so long for its dagger

so long as you keep my dagger on loan
it's not the silk in between
but your absence that grows old

Translated by Şehnaz Tahir Gürçağlar
from Once a Tailor (1995)

Carry Us Across!

they pity us a lot here
we're so naked even our wound
is healed in an other, in vain we hide
in the relief the fallen find in us
wherever we go, a city, to whomever
we go a distance remains within

cast off your lines into our abyss
look how our borders merge as if
like our scents they change who the apple
who the dreadfully ill and who
tossed in his own boat from one shore
to another of his mind

so right through the middle my
mind a split apple: face to face
its gardens, in one hard, soft in the other
O my mind don't come out even if I say apple!
O the nakedness that pacifies the suns
above, half as I am far from the scent
of my mind still in your gardens
I should've been you, to be more,
to pay off your debt to the future,
cast off my lines, let my mind
unfurl its sail, the wind is within me,
cast off my lines, the more
we drift away from each other, the more
we are bound together,
cast off my lines!

your boat has time yet to ply onward and back,
its load not the old wine, not the black olive
not the fig jealous of the tasty lie
fallen from illusion into our garden
to your boat that heavy apple's a burden

carry us across, filled with words
you called for your boat we arrived, filled with pleasure
you uprooted your gardens we arrived, filled with migration
you betrayed your tongue we arrived, filled with traces
whitenesses covet our dreams

carry us across
this is an apple gone out of its mind
whose garden is uprooted
don't take us into your boat,

carry us across in you!

Translated by İpek Seyalıoğlu and Mel Kenne
from Once a Tailor (1995)

Pomegranate

Winter looms large, let's head for the pomegranate
day's face turns chilly, let's go for the pomegranate
it may just have something to say and offer us
a thousand-and-one warm words about summer
our tongue is dry, let's get out of here
and go to the pomegranate, a household so populous
I wish we lived there too
this house looms large, every room
a parting, every child a box shut fast,
gardens unkempt: once sharing a bunch of grapes
we were such friends, gardens and vines,
but a thief unseen was already stripping the garden
of its green, leaving the vines bare!
If a rough hand enters the pomegranate's garden
poverty strikes the tongue first, then the flesh
so before the tongue chills and flesh feels the hurt
let's head for the pomegranate for a lusty revelation;
a house like the pomegranate, garden within a garden,
a woman the garden for love, crazy ivy
let's cling to her love, let's set off for the pomegranate now.

Let's say from the fiery pomegranate we plucked that love.

Translated by Saliha Paker
from Forty Poems and One (1997)

19

Cardboard Suitcase

again a paper winter and cardboard suitcase
you're like locals who think the cherry a fruit

'Alice in the Cities' a remote child
is our new captain: hey out there
we've got lots of water here, too,
don't forget to bring your ships when you come!

I guess the sea fits some cities
like a word stuck in the wrong language,
missionaries seem to take the orange away
any child whose dreams are robbed
from other children would be remote

I guess the orange is the reason
why the child has lost himself homesick for the cherry

they think the child is ill, that when he passes
under the moon, he'll turn blond
the child has his stars, I guess, and his garden, too,
if only they'd give him some water there
and launch his cherryship in the desert inside him…

I guess you didn't see the desert for the sandstorm
a pity, we hadn't seen a stranger for so long
even Alice had come, the sea was translated
to a foreign tongue, the child wore a blond mask
was going to forgive the orange,
if the salt between your two lips
hadn't collected so much in your words
the wind would've blown twice in the same sentence
and the second time blown the poem off the paper

don't take the cardboard suitcase on the ship,
sail off to the cherry! remote child
go to the city and sing us all!

*Translated by Mel Kenne and Saliha Paker
from* Hafız and Salamander (2002)

Letter to God

1.

I just saw the clouds
start to pile up in the sky, God
and I saw that you're
writing a poem in secret

2.

I think of you sometimes
God, it grieves me.
Cats, birds, clouds,
trees, grass, fish,
girls, boys, children,
if you only were theirs alone,
not the God of the whole
great humankind!

3.

In civil war
God is killed first
then the good people
among us

4.

My God, so many trees
you've got here,
and so many people
who say 'in this world
there's not even
one tree I planted
for myself'

If you ever decide
to create another tree,
please let it be
a Human Tree!

5.

Forgive me, God
when I look at those hyena types
I can't believe certain people
were created by you

6.

The clouds you've shown me,
God, an artist has seen them too
and thought you were an artist!

7.

Wise enough to stay in this world,
nomadic enough to risk life,
in search of a pearl and deep
enough to get lost in the self,
and intense enough to gush out
even after a brief allusion to water…

What are humans, if not
masters at waving goodbye
to everything before they lose it?

But God, I guess you'd
waved goodbye to us
even before we did!

8.

When a village burns
the silence of the world dies

the whispering of kissing dies
when a forest burns up

when they burn down a hotel
the guestwork of poetry dies

the laughter of childhood dies
when a city's burnt down

Whoever sets life on fire,
God will set their hearts
in ice

9.

God, either forget you've created this world
or don't leave me in this world so forgotten!

Translated by İpek Seyalıoğlu
from Hafız and Salamander (2002)

We're Lonely, Brother Cemal

This rakı, Cemal my brother
you know, drinking this rakı with you
was like going to Kars

In your poems, how we would drink rakı
for hours, you know, Cemal my brother,
we would go to Kars for ages

You know, after you, Cemal my brother
no poem goes to Kars
Kars is brief, rakı tasteless
in poetry, after you,
everything hits bottom
see how lonely we are

Translated by Elizabeth Pallitto and Arzu Eker Roditakis
from Hafız and Salamander (2002)

Borrowed Like Sorrow

Once poetry was like my dog
able to sense my sadness
and so take its place at my side

Now my poetry's an old hound
grown deaf, its heart deadened

*

I was so wounded back then
only an animal could've felt for me

If I've learned anything from animals
it's that I know nothing at all about humans

And so I saw: each human needs an animal

*

Some pick their words off of trees
some grind their poetry from stone
their love from the desert...
I from none of them

My feeling is that I belong to night
that there's a roadhouse and that
I'm a poet who's ended up inside it

What's mine isn't poetry or sorrow
if I could only find the shadow they left behind
that would be enough for me

*

Inside you, a street winding down to the sea
inside me, a house leading to the capital city

old fumes, old coal, old rails
a beautiful darkness once ran between us

*

When rain comes, poets need to be called up
and asked about the apple, about its secret,
if not, the apple, the secret, the poet
all must be forgotten with the rain, and *nothing
asked of all those who stay silent*

There's an apple I owe you, but
the apple alone knows this, not you

*

The sorrow of words seems to be made of paper
the pain of emptiness wrought more finely than a sentence

The sorrow of a tree is made of its leaves
loves are levelled before the *gazel*

The sorrow of the rain is what it murmurs
when an orphan falls into its wooden abode

Love's sorrow is like that of a tenant
homeless if he leaves before settling down
displaced if he's settled

Apart from poetry I have no other sorrow

There's no train in the poem
So why all this grief?

*

Each new issue from poetry journals
is like grief's final print run

*

You know how, like animals
just before they die, one wants to hide away
a person needs a place to go hide
in love, in childhood, to a mother, in poetry
otherwise death would overcome us
and we'd die incomplete

*

Observing the water I want to overflow
the water has a glass but I've got no one

...

Some other line would've been here but
the water took over my mind, I forgot

*

In our midst are these eyes
Hasan's eyes
Selahattin's eyes
Ece's eyes
I was talking to Seyhan
and when, nearing the end,
his father wore a stare like Ece's,
as if pleading 'don't leave me'
like my father too, looking back on his childhood

Roaming through our souls are eyes
don't crash into them as you look
don't shatter them as you pass by
those eyes are our poetry
our toasty bread
what's left from childhood
both father and son, those eyes

*

I saw how when a mother wept
a child grew up
when an animal cried
I heard the trees complaining

Mountains rising steeply
there's a certain feeling in that

*

Rather than wonder which lie to believe
one comes finally to believe in belief alone
and in the end not a single lie is left
except for the thought that everything is real

*

In the old script
'face' when written meant a picture
'eye' when written meant love
and a 'word' when written was poetry
so some relationship must exist
between writing 'fall' and the heart
and writing 'summer' and childhood

*

Mornings are tough
much more so than poetry

*

I couldn't take my friend a rose for fear of spoiling him

Translated İdil Karacadağ and Mel Kenne
from Borrowed Like Sorrow (2005)

29

Lost Brother

To Şahin Şencan

O God, my landlord, let me
live in your house a little longer
within me the brother I carry is alone
once I give birth to him, I won't stay here

O my brother, my street, let me
carry you within me a little longer
once you set out on your own,
I'll be all alone in the world

O my lifetime, my little room, let me
seek a path in poetry a little longer
if soul coincides, may I find the many
lost brothers I have on this path

Translated by Arzu Eker Roditakis and Elizabeth Pallitto
from Borrowed Like Sorrow (2005)

II.

Gazel of Secrets

like a cedar I come from the East of love
in the East there's a love crossed like a desert

if I crossed, I'd be crossed, I'd smile and catch fire

all I didn't have I left at a shop called the world
no one to claim the goods, only wounding words

were I silent, I'd be queried, I'd speak and catch fire

as for the secret of the wine, I'm an abandoned inn
useless to fume, the world's a wreck of souls

if I opened up, I'd be shut down, I'd dry out and catch fire

at the four gates I turned cloud, a mirror deceived me
a mirror that can't keep its silver wears a dark face

if I looked, I'd be crushed, I'd fall and catch fire

when your hope in me died, I let you loose in the world
since our discourse died, I've been diving deeper and deeper

as a novice I only shed tears, now I'm on fire inside out

Translated by Clifford Endres and Selhan Savcıgil-Endres
from Sorrowful Cats *Gazel* (2007)

Gazel of Idylls

as if you'd just left the rain, your eyes
so childlike, so warm, so wide

you must be a town or a pomegranate
maybe Granada, maybe September, maybe red

what is your body if not your soul's summer night
most idyllic, most windy, most sea-like

you childishly fell in love again
as if with me, as if… oh! as if it can be

even love fails to fill some lovers' place
so that praise, so that to you, so that in June

when desire's asleep the soul wanders all naked
hence the *gazel*, hence the sorrow, hence the secret

as if you'd just left the town, your eyes
so chatty, so shy, ready to cry

now go! find new towns of this love and ruin them for our hearts

Translated by Gökçenur Ç.
from Sorrowful Cats *Gazel* (2007)

Gazel of Orphans

love is for those who have a heart, fearful are those
with hearts as big as a dove, for the heart is fragile

forgotten is the pomegranate, broken is the wing, suppose
water is less deep than blood poisoned with speech

My brother Hrant, my pomegranate flame, I was richer
with you until my heart was broken again

me in the *semah* of cranes, you in the dance of doves,
we'd be a poem at the *cem* rite of blues, so the dream goes

a man's country is his friend, so I've learned, God, too,
didn't He create the world to be His friend?

a country dies with each friend, with each teardrop
so does God again, and a thousand cranes with each dove...

in truth we are neither Turks, nor Kurds, nor Armenians,
ours such a 'father,' Hrant, we are all orphans

heartbroken, like a pomegranate not split open we're orphans

Translated by Nilgün Dungan and Arzu Akbatur
from Sorrowful Cats *Gazel* (2007)

Inner *Nefes*

she ordered a tea, on the train
we were passengers, in the desert
I'd been left alone, within you
and yet how many others had I pushed aside to love you!

we've passed by love, you can open your eyes now

she'd taken shelter in language, in one of its words
her path crossed mine, in the desert
I was worn out, within you
and yet in how many children did I praise instead of you!

we've passed by the dream, you can look at yourself now

she'd broken down in me alone, well within me
and staked her vast pavilion within my soul
who was I good for now, within you
and yet how many gardens did I neglect tending you!

who have we passed by? ask anyone

*Translated by Caroline Stockford and Selhan Savcıgil-Endres
from* Sorrowful Cats *Gazel* (2007)

Gone Quiet *Nefes*

before you even existed I was mad at you
the lack of you upset me, and then you were here
you were so beautiful I could not want you for myself
now I'm subdued by your absence as if you were here

this sensitivity, oh, you can't imagine
things that should upset me seem to make no mark at all
what am I to do, your presence is more desolate than your absence
have you left me no one else to go quiet on
I alone am left in the desert of your silence

I know you won't offer the silent treatment to just anyone
and your eyes are like autumn, that stealer of leaves
as memories fall, eyes will fill
those eyes must be cleaned before summer is here
or the silence between us will be sullied by tears

you must love someone enough to go quiet on them
don't talk when they arrive: where were you all this time?
why didn't you love me?
without you I had no one not to talk to
is what you should say
and when they're with you, never go quiet on anyone

Translated by Caroline Stockford and Selhan Savcıgil-Endres
from Sorrowful Cats *Gazel* (2007)

Write a Letter

'Write a letter, let your habits be renewed'
writes Sheikh Galip, I reaffirm my master's words:
write a letter, let your soul catch fire
write a letter, let your anger cool down
write a letter, let your inner self return
write a letter, so your tea is refreshed in Erzurum
write a letter, so your breath is revived at Tahtakuşlar village
Mahzunî Şerif the bard, Ali Ekber Çiçek, you write a letter too
Haydar Haydar, write a letter, so your childhood comes back to you
write a letter, Grand Arcade, Arjantin beer, Tanju Okan
write a letter, let Ankara come here at once
write a letter, aunt Kadriye, brother Mehmet, bald Hasan
write a letter, *The Garden of Departed Cats*: Blacky, Fishbones, Sweetcorn
to the long hot provincial summers, write a letter
write a letter, water birds, hills of love
afternoons with mama, mornings with nana, write a letter
the streets of brotherhood in an old town, write a letter
write a letter in the shadeless yellow heat of patience
write a letter, in times of waiting its shadow will suffice
write a letter, write, write, write – let them all come to you!
(*write a letter, ……………. fill in the blanks yourself!*)

...

write a letter, so communism comes to Turkey this winter
write a letter, tell it not to show its face in Ankara
tell it to wait for me at the gates of Youth Park
Communism is the Turkic world's biggest enemy
wherever it rears its ugly head it must be crushed
let's meet under that sign, we won't arouse any suspicion
write a letter, not once did you visit us, so very ungrateful
no, don't call it ungrateful, that would be rude, write instead,
you made us miss you so much, are we so easy to forget?
some reproach is good, it shows how much we care
say, we've got tired of having our eyes glued to the road

are you never going to arrive at all?
write a letter, try to soften its heart a little, to win its favour
do something, anything, only please make it reach here
say, those who love you in this land have aged for lack of you
write a letter, no need for a visa anymore, don't linger at the border
you can stay for up to ninety days in Turkey
the rest is up to you, but you're more than welcome here
you can spend a whole lifetime, in Antalya, by the Mediterranean
in five star hotels if you wish, don't worry, it's all inclusive
write a letter, write for it to arrive by summer, tell it not to wait for winter
if it likes it here, it can settle down, take up permanent residence
but make sure you don't email it, or call its mobile, then it won't come
write a letter, if communism is meant to reach this country after all
it'll have to come by post; if letters ever do arrive, of course
but don't worry about that, you still write
at least tell it we're here, waiting eagerly, always expectant
write a letter, since no one else is anticipating their arrival
and neither a letter nor communism have anywhere else to go
write a letter, so they can both spend their days of retirement
in this heavenly country, bordered on three sides by the sea!

Translated by İdil Karacadağ
from Envelope (2011)

Amor Fati

It's not only my two days that are like each other
if I had two lives they'd be like each other too
even if they weren't who cares I'd make them alike anyway
even if I were two I would be like the other, because I wouldn't know
what to do with the other, if, say, I had two hearts
even though one is sometimes too much, God bless it,
their fate would also be to become alike, as if to be each other's
fate they would also remain inside me, how would I know
if it were good, let's say it was, what a two-timist I am,
like *amor fati, amor fati*, love your fate, love your fate,
I would tell both my hearts to be my fate, be my fate
before they unite, forget me in a corner, and call it fate!

Translated by Arzu Akbatur and Mel Kenne
from An Anthology of Love Poems (2011)

Where Do Your Eyes Come From?

Where have you come from?
– From the river!
But why are your eyes not green
it seems that the river hasn't flowed from your eyes
your eyes never looked in the river
the river never looked in your eyes
or perhaps you have never looked inside yourself
it seems you left nothing of your eyes in the river
had you cried on its bank your tears would have mingled
and your eyes made peace with the river
but you haven't glanced at its waters
you left it not one *gazel* from your autumn
nor even one lotus flower from your bliss
it seems you've left your inner source as dry as a well
your eyes have not dived in the depths of a river.

A river's made not only of its flowing, it has shadow
an eye is made not only of seeing, but its shadow
you've never let your eyelashes unfurl in the shade
for lashes need coolness, they lengthen in the cool,
while your eyes are so sun-filled, so bare, full of glances
they might have calmed with the mercy of your lashes,
had you looked in the river your eyes may have been lulled,
even the shadow of the river may have stilled your eyes
for them to be healed, be able to see night, to see within you,
your lashes could have fallen into the well of dreams
from the nakedness of your tear-dried eyes,
from your sleeplessness devoid of dreams.

You must have looked not in a river, but a well
as rivers are plumbed with sight, and wells with sound
people get a darkblack voice from gazes deep as wells
it seems the river never passed through your eyes
not even the shadow of the river passed through,

your eyes seem to have plummeted into a well,
people's eyes take their colour from things that they love
from love, from the river, from olives, from grapes, from shadows
had your eyes come from the river
your soul would have looked at me
if from the river your eyes had come
they would have flowed into me
we would have flowed into each other...

...

Your eyes do not come from the river
perhaps from solitude
perhaps from a wasteland
perhaps from desolation
maybe your eyes
come from your tears...

Translated by Caroline Stockford
from An Anthology of Love Poems (2011)

A Guide to the Preservation of Fall

Fall paused on the lakeshore
silence a swan multiplied by two...
now an extra leaf perhaps
falls from memory ...

that's how I started a poem

Who stays behind
in fellowship, passion, separation
his name turns to fall
— her name is written as fall — is also possible

it could have gone on like this
and an old fall have ended up
once more as this poem

As a leaf-thief in September I congratulate myself
in fall-dried lines like these:

If like a leaf
humanity falls from itself
fall ah
who from whom is saved?

What fall said to the leaf, the leaf to the poem:
humanity too must know how to fall from itself

Translated by Clifford Endres and Selhan Savcıgil-Endres
from An Anthology of Love Poems (2011)

Preface to Love

Don't upset me

Don't upset yourself over me either

Don't let our promises grow cold

Don't go too far away from me

Don't go too far into me either

Nor go too far into yourself

So far as to be lost within

Send roses to the past

Don't forget

Memories grow thirsty too

Take good care of them

Take care of me

Hold me

Hang on to me

Don't leave me here or there

With this one or that one

Do not forget

Listen

Translated by Clifford Endres and Selhan Savcıgil-Endres
from An Anthology of Love Poems (2011)

Blue It Was…

Such a summer it was
as if we lived in the sky

To kiss you was like kissing the sky
it was something blue

Youth is just such a summer
no dorm no home no room
the sky alone
enough for anyone

You and I we lived
so much in the sky
our youth
blue it was … so very blue!

Translated by Nilgün Dungan and Mel Kenne
from An Anthology of Love Poems (2011)

The Kid with the Green Shirt

I'm not a poet nor is this a poem
I'm writing on behalf of that kid with the green shirt
others don't see his green shirt
he can't show the heart inside his green shirt
he's upset
'never mind' they say 'no rush
'there are plenty more days
you can put on your green shirt again,
keep your heart pure'
The main thing I wonder
is who spoke that last sentence:
Keep your heart pure!

He keeps his heart pure
so well that everyone laughs at him
even from inside his shirt
the green-shirted kid's heart can be seen
this time he'd like to hide his heart
but he doesn't know where
a kid who's never hid his heart before
how could he know
he wants to hold it in his palm
as he held a sparrow when small
and felt its heart in his palm
the heart may be something like that
as small as your palm
small enough to be held in your palm
nobody even wants to borrow it
ah if a child can't even
lend out his heart
how could he live with it
he has no idea ... nor do I...

From some of his friends
who don't wear green shirts
he hears 'my heart was broken'
instead of that green shirt
he'd like to wear that sentence
he could give away his green shirt
just to be able to say it
no one breaks his heart
no one knows his heart

The kid with the green shirt
does he have no heart?
show us your heart
if he does, where is it?
green-shirted kid
show us your heart!

...

The kid's name is Beşir
he's got a green shirt on
a poem left by Turgut Uyar

...

Wearing that green shirt
he always changes, sure,
but always wearing it
does he have to stay
the same kid inside?
people may think
it's all the same,
if not the green one
the blue one will be
just fine on him they'll say

...

So look, now you see why
I wrote this poem on the behalf
of that kid with the green shirt
I'm quite a bit older than he is of course
I mean my time to become a poet is past
but the green-shirted kid is at poetry's prime
he thinks his shirt holds the secrecy of his heart
there's something I need to say but can't
I can put on a green shirt in his place
I can write a poem in his place
I can suffer in his place
but more than that I don't know

I love that kid with the green shirt
I'd like him not to show his heart no
let them steal his heart
let him have no heart
these days a heart's not a must
it's superfluous
I don't want to write anything
more about the heart now
not for him or for me
besides nobody saw the heart
he bore inside the green shirt,
didn't even hear his poem once
I'm cutting that kid out of this poem
I'm taking the green shirt off the kid
the poem and the shirt are yours now
whether it's blue now or black or red
whoever's shirt is open to summer
keep writing, wandering, loving
just keep far away from that kid's heart!

Translated by Mel Kenne and Nilgün Dungan
from An Anthology of Love Poems (2011)

47

I Could Never Be An Evening!

I could never be an evening, I could never be solitude
don't trust me, you shouldn't risk leaping off my cliff
because it's neither deep nor full of imagery, not even one line grows there,
and if you do, you'll only be left with your dreams shattered,
fractured into pieces, yet soon you'll wake up from those too
but don't worry, afterwards nothing worse can happen to you!
I told you, with me time passes lightly, soft as *thefoamoftheday*
and if I cry, it's only because I occasionally get soap in my eye!
Even my train is built out of wood, you set out for a journey in it
and it's like carrying your entire house around with you, it's not
always the customer that is right but sometimes the shopkeeper is too
the train gets bored of me quickly, in the same way that my house does
like a lengthy period of unemployment not a word is ever said between us
if I were to linger longer the wooden train would break in half with tedium!
My nights are short too, this is why my dreams are uninterpreted
let's not bring the days into this, they pass me by in the blink of an eye
much in the way they start out or without even starting at all
I've gone on a bit again, so here is what I wanted to tell you in a line or two:
'*You my offbeat, oddball darling*
How quickly evening has descended unnoticed
I wanted to say that, but I'm not called Attila İlhan and this is no evening
and I know where this is going: 'how this turned into a poem unnoticed'
but I will not say it, won't let myself bring that line into this
I love a bit of Haydar and a bit of Ergülen poetry
and the evening and you too, but I also know myself
I'm not the writer of unforgettable love poems
I told you before, that's Attila İlhan, but how good that you came
bringing a bit of poetry and a bit of the evening with you
what if I go and get my first sweetheart from Beşiktas too?

Translated by İdil Karacadağ
from An Anthology of Love Poems (2011)

And She Says:

within is a silence that mingles with water and runs on
ticking like clockwork
she says: I like studious silences
silence is flowing between us

If you wish I can change the lights
for the light of our union shines only in our eyes
the light of separation may blind us
is evening light coming from morning or noon
what difference is there – no one may know

Love is for indulging your loved one alone
It spoils you and lets you be spoilt
and the afterward is bathed in soothing affection

she says: others' solitude would not scare us so
if we knew how to be guests in our own.

Translated by Caroline Stockford
from An Anthology of Love Poems (2011)

Love is Small

you line up the whole world in front of me
and I'm afraid
because the world is larger than love
old maps, old geographies
past empires, past loves
I am scared
an imperial reign is too long for love
if it's as long as a republic that's enough

Despite this world I do…
love you but
I want to tell a lie too
about love not being of this world
saying something like:
'Love is another geography
and no map marks its place'
I can even exaggerate a bit more:
'love, despite the both of us,
is an empire built for two'

Go now, straight back
to yourself and enter your heart
love is not something that knows no bounds
it does have its surface, mass and square metres
sometimes it's the size of a house, sometimes a street
there are times it's considered a park, bridge or passage
all in all it is narrower than this world

Yes, it is love that sets up a home
I have a room there of my own
and its door is open to you as long as
you don't set up the house in between you and me
then I will tell you that the house is us
and that I have no other home but you

let's live way up on the sixth floor – it's only love, you know
let's not even have an elevator
love shouldn't be reached that easily
we will name it '*chaine-des-coeurs*'
isn't there a creeping plant called that
we didn't reach this love by elevator
we climbed to this love step by step
let us say

yes my darling
our love is smaller than the world
to know this would serve humanity well
let's not fool anyone and never each other
the world's no good to us, a house would suit us fine
the world is larger than love
even if the world is vast, and the house is small
let our hearts move in there first
let our love fill a three-bedroomed place
that's enough for me!

*Translated by Caroline Stockford and Arzu Akbatur
from* An Anthology of Love Poems (2011)

Engaged Words

I'll rinse off your voice like an apple
I'll buff up your words like grapes
I'll praise you with perfumed speech
I'll drop myself off in the waves of the desert
I'll swim for you in its bluest sands
I'll fly in my mind for you
I'll be Sindbad, Aladdin, 1001 Nights for you
a mule for you, for you an Arab horse
a red-maned horse and until I burst
I'll bellow out I love you with foaming words
for you I'll forget everything I know
and then I'll relearn it all just for you
I'll shut my eyes to memories for you
and I'll start to see again with your eyes
thus with love too I'll declare to all that for the engaged
it so happens that love is the longest syllable,
and with awe I'll spell out love
that to be engaged means only to spell
the syllable I'll never forget, like a pinky
my pinky, my engagement finger, my syllable
my betrothed, like a syllable I'll wear you on my sparrow finger
let's turn ourselves into sparrows, never grow,
turn one another into glass, never break,
from two halves never become a whole, be syllabic
your milk I'll spell too and like milk drink your pains
like sand I'll love you in the moment of heat
like a mountain I'll revere you
I'll face onto you like a courtyard
in summer and winter flow like a river
I'll be seen to your eyes as in a *cem* rite
I'll be your suitor, in your presence supplicate
for you I'll lead cranes toward merriment
for you I'll lead horses toward poems
for you I'll gather jade from the wilderness

and only for you I'll await you
and I'll await the night for you to come
will wait for you to open like a door
and for you will strip words naked from head to toe
for you I'll leave the poem stark naked
no metre no rhyme no refrain no image
no music no harmony no rhythm no tone
no epic no lyric no space no word
both the Muse and the bemusing, engaged one, are you
like a desert, a Bedouin, an Arabian poet
like the Arabian poetry tradition in sandy light
in seven nights I'll write your poem
and in syllabic desert metre love you sevenfold

Translated by Mel Kenne and Nilgün Dungan
from An Anthology of Love Poems (2011)

Translation

Translation is now a must for the old body
whose sense is so obscure in the new language
in the old one a many-layered word would clothe us
in the new one, just throw the word away for all to see!
Words too go quiet on the body as it falls into need
and feels cold without even a comma to cover it,
the flesh unable to find its being in a sentence
also forgets to transcend itself like the spirit…
If only one knew that the body was built willfully
and that the spirit laughed like a playful neighbour,
even joking about it would horrify the body,
now all is shadow except the flesh!
O spirit, old torch, say when your sea
will open out to this ship of modern times,
words are drowning one by one like old friends
is there any spirit left in the deep to pull them out?
In their eyes my spirit lies still like an inland sea
and my body like a lake, all closed in,
they took my little rowing boat far out on the water
and said, 'untie your ropes,' but I'm empty inside, nothing more…

For one who can't swim in spirit could the body ever be a shore?

Translated by Saliha Paker
from An Anthology of Love Poems (2011)

III.

On Things That Are Falling Asleep

The girls have calmed, their breasts like a millpond.

The twenties were sunny but I forgot what the thirties were like
I could never forget just how scarlet the twenties were
passionate, fiery, sweaty and self-assured
courageous, red-eyed, and fast enough to pass right through themselves
that's how the twenties went by, they lasted long – say, another twenty years
this is why when I think of the thirties longtwenties come to my mind

Yet I would have expected you to pick up what others forgot
so only you would remember, instead of everyone, yes, that was you
you were Turkey's scrapbook or something of the sort anyway
that's what I thought — he'd never forget, he wou ldnev erforget, he'dne verfor get
that is why I expected it of you, you were there because of it, that's all
that is why I was for you, that is why we were all for one another
there were forty of us all apart but our one concern was Turkey
from poor birds to scattered islands to the pigeons, and more besides…
(*I think I'm getting tired of writing poems I can't stand myself writing poetry even as I'm*
writing it, this is why the poems are getting longer, and I'm tired of words too,
and having to create things out of them…)

Everybody keeps going on about Turkey in their poetry, so here's a version from me:
white Turkey, black Turkey, green Turkey and there's the Kızılbaş too
their Turkey is inner Turkey, poetry leads onto a street called Turkey or something
I haven't even left my house yet, much less poetry, I've not even looked
out of the window – be careful, what if Turkey sees you!
I've just said the twenties, but there are the thirties and the forties yet to come,
and Turkey's still on the horizon, waiting for them all…
when I think of Turkey, I think of none of you, nonemost of you, nonepoetry of you
you're waving around your poems and your rhymes like flags for nothing,
sit down! Turkey, you sit down too, when I think of Turkey
only Cemal Süreya comes to my mind and he never, ever leaves
I swear Cemal Süreya is my Turkey, everyone stirs ashes but let's stir rain for once
perhaps the rain is a consolation for the ashes of the poet

I remember now, the thirties were a wildfire, we're still sitting on the ashes
would that steady streams of shame rain down, for as loooong as the longtwenties!

Thirties! They were just like God 'stirring up the old seas'
could I ever forget them, yes I could, I could forget the girls too
and their breasts too, what about the poets you say, well I forgot them long ago
the girls soon run out of milk, they get old before the poets do,
perhaps the lines written for the girls by the poets remain,
we love some poets because we take them for a poem, we remember them as a poem,
their poetry might not be as tragic as their childhood, we love them for their childhood,
we think maybe their poetry is just as full of sleep as their childhood
we love the poem staring at us right in the eye *with the joy / of there being no sleep
beneath anybody's eyelids,* and besides we think that if the poem is full of sleep then
it must be full of dreams too, so we want to love it once more for that and we do,
I've loved Cemal Süreya too not as a city but as a neighbourhood
like I've loved Eskişehir, which is my oldest neighbourhood, my childhood,
my childcity, like Odunpazarı, Yoğurtçu Park, Kadıköy, Eyüp, Emirgân, Kuzguncuk
like Cebeci used to be, because I've come to think that anything I love, I love
because of its eyes, I love love because of its eyes, and drinking water too
even saying I love you because of its eyes, and lyrical cities too, which could be called
feminine neighbourhoods, even poetry because of its eyes, in short
what I love the most are things that are falling asleep,
three cheers for the city but let the neighbourhood be sleepy, let the breasts of the girls
be covered, so they become pensive, pensive because of their gaze
let them fill up, dive in, overflow – let them open, close, then stay asleep until morning
let them remain half open like eyelids do, let the letters of the words be covered too,
for they are the ones who train their gaze on the distance the most
small letters, big letters, black, white, horizontal, slanted, vertical, thin, tall, thick, short
but don't let the pages accuse them of sleeplessness, sleep is milk
sleep is a lake of beauty, it means dreaming in warm milk; it means rejoicing in milk
sleep overflows from milk, as the lake too overflows from beauty, sleep is poetry's milk
that is my sole reason for liking poetry from now on, lately it's been getting sleepy
it's been too sleepy too often, drinking the milk of an incomplete childhood after years,
gulping it down – staring into the milky depths even as it's downing it
even now its letters are about to shut their eyes
each of the eyes gazes more wistfully than the others…

I would never forget Cemal Süreya, but there is something bothering this poem
I wonder if he hadn't said anything about the tail end of the thirties
say, something about the lives of four swallows, one of them on the face of the sky
the other that one's shadow, another one searching the waters for the swiftly gone by
days of its youthful flights, as if it'd dropped one of its wings, and yet another –
no matter how many swallows it ends up being, he has no other life than poetry, pity
this is what one should say, even if it's base to say so: at the end of everything,
a person should be told 'he had no other poem but his life'
a man is what his end becomes: 'we took him for a poem!'
we took poetry to be a dream with a milky shadow
we took it to be the middle of a sleep whose shadow falls into milk…

The thirties must have been rocky, the summer wind or the moonlit waters of the sea
would be too romantic in comparison – to describe it one should start with the
    four winds and then move on to a rainstorm, a tornado, a hurricane
I know about the forties, they were full of rain that one thought would never end,
like a steady downpour which looked as if it would stay with you forever,
as if you'd be washed with the same water when you die: the world is not permanent
the world is full of rain, and at that moment, I stood between the world and the rain
if not during the twenties then during the thirties I had my fair share of the black sun
I had heard it called melancholy, Süha Tuğtepe called it 'melancholia' and whenever I
heard him say it I beamed with admiration, thinking 'that is such a Süha type of word'
if there is a single trace of friendship left in this world it's mostly down to him
and now I want to catch up with my breath before the words mingle with the rain
so I have to tell you what I would have said at the end
out of breath and before it gets too late…

When the girls calmed down and certain things started falling asleep
I had been waiting in a house with a view of the sea (cf. 'Kuzguncuk Hotel', my old
poem, my old home) I should correct that and say 'a house by the sea', actually
seeing how I'm writing a poem, I could even say 'a house on the sea'
I could say all these and so much more…
the sea had its own colour, back then I couldn't decide whether to stay or to leave
whether to flow or stand still, was I even alive those days?
no, I was merely living, I was caught in-between, in-between everything
the sea made me think of eternity and maybe that is the reason why

I thought my home was meant to be a hotel, as for myself, a refugee
whose only desire is to stay one more day, one more night
are we not all transitory compared to the sea?
we are shackled to the moment, the sea flows freely
we are impermanent, the sea exists eternally

I wonder if the sea and I were a bit too close back then
once more I didn't know something that everyone else did, the sea was blue
really, the girls were blue too, and I suspect from the way this line is going
you expect me to write that their breasts were blue as well, but
I didn't know then that blue was a name for girls who didn't exist
that this meant something like 'saudade': the blue girl is not here
(cf. my poem called 'Le Poete Regarde' that is 'The Poet Watches')
I think the letters of sleep are blue like the letters of milk
so is that why your eyelids descend upon the gloom
heavy as the birds of old but with wings as light as feathers

Neither our sleep nor our letters are blue
as if all that falls to our share are just words
the sea ebbs, the blue leaves, what's left to us are their letters
bitterness ebbs, gets up and leaves, what's left to us are its sighs:
the world is darkness my friends
the world is a huge house full of gloom
the world is only what the eye perceives
the eye that doesn't gaze at the world gazes into the gloom
your eyes well up because of the world
we were born for our eyes (were we not?)
did our eyes not dive into the lake of bitterness, for all the searching they did?
I myself had an episode of gentleness, and even if back then I called the world
a well of sadness, I now declare it to be a well of bitterness

A pit of gloom, a pit within, sleep is a pit full of warmth
the abyss is sleep; and just like day and night
sleep and the abyss are as deep as each other, contained within each other
how strange it is – the world seems to exist just so it can be talked about
that is all it seems to be there for, and is the poet not one who gives up poetry

when he realises this, whereas those like me with the zeal of a newcomer
become enchanted with the magic of their own invention and thus,
by which I mean, by keeping on writing
they write and they write only to lose the poetry of the world
if poetry exists on earth, if the earth itself has a poem
it's the poets who are responsible for the loss of it…

The pit of gloom is the pit within one's self
after the gloom, what more can fall into the abyss within me?
the well inside me is dark, dark pit, within me is darkness
darkblackwellblacksleepdark…
I came down from my eyes right before sleep arrived
the night hadn't found where my eyes were yet
and I was still one of those who had longer days than nights
which meant I was from longdaysland
which meant inside me I was still naked
it was in the way I would greet a certain person
saying something like 'may your day be longer than your night'
he would repeat the sentiment in turn: yours too
when I would have expected him to say 'may your night be the same'
he wouldn't say it, it's what we always did
and in this way we would repeat the world over and over again…

The sea had its own colour, back then I was in the midst of
a way of living like *Dirty August,* I was on the shore of a sea
I was in a pit of hell, not deep down but at the very bottom
infinity turned greyer and greyer, sometimes it became the very image of August
all around was a scent of not-white, I smelt it, the odour of dirtiness
whereas infinity had a smell of blue, I understood it even if I didn't see it

It was at the end of the thirties, the times were rough; and I was quite down
I was out in the open, far away from it all, from the shore, from the sea, from the
    blueness
far from the earth, far from my inner self, far from poetry, I wanted it all to stop
I wanted the sea to stand still like a stretch of blue earth, completely flat
I wanted the waves to be creaseless, as if they'd just been ironed out

they could stand still forever and I could sleep
as if I had a wharf within me and could doze forever in the blueness of the sea
anchored to it until I lose at the end
both the colour of infinity and its scent…

I had moored myself to a house which I took for a hotel
back then neither the girls nor the sea were blue…
like infinity, that is, the colour of what doesn't exist
blue for me is more of a smell than a colour
infinity too, is a passage of time
they say both the letters of sleep and its smell are blue
I learnt it well, the world is a house of gloom
sleep is the alphabet of rain
rain is a well of sleep

The world exists just so it can be said it exists
why does desire exist
it exists for those whom the world holds in its thrall
desire means accepting an invitation issued by the world

As I was writing this poem on things that are falling asleep
I suddenly realised I wanted to write never-ending poems
in my own handwriting, as Cherry my cat, slumbered on the page
the house and its cat asleep on the poem, on the letters of the words
the sleep of paper, the sleep of letters, Cherry's sleep
this is a memory in which it seems like even the abyss is sleepy
I knew this to be so before I had written it, before I even had a cat
before the shadow of sleep fell onto the paper
before the shadows of sleepy letters fell onto the poem
I can't decide whether we throw the letters onto the page or into it
would that I could write, forget what I've written, then start rewriting
write on haphazardly so poems could remain for me forever as drafts
so I could write nothing but drafts, in the same way I'm writing this poem
would that I could stop myself from tinkering with it, from rewriting it
would that both the original and the proof were this, and I could just send it off
away from inside me, away from my inclinations, simply a page with a pure heart…

Would that this poem weren't refined – no aesthetic interventions, no plastic concerns
would that it could stay unspoiled, unprocessed and rough around the edges
would that it were a pure poem, a fat poem, a long poem, a loose poem,
a boring poem, an abundant poem, a narrow poem, a saggy poem, a thin poem,
an old poem, a way-past-its-time poem, an elderly poem, an archaic poem,
a badly-timed poem or even a sleepy poem…
for poems too can fall asleep!

And now I'm saying it too at last, *poeta pirata est*
the poet is a pirate, we could even call him a thief
after all both a pirate and a thief disdain private property
and the place of the poet should be somewhere between the two
he should borrow both the words and the poem itself
as the world is poetry's garden too, his long-gone childhood calls on him
to break into the garden

…

It seems somebody's sleep ran away with the world, and so he thinks
those who forgot their eyes on this earth can be freed of this pit of gloom
and have fun on their own for a little while and some more…
(*I actually like writing poems, there are a thousand reasons for it*
at the start one doesn't know what to write at all
travelling, marvellous tramping around, Oh my heart, leaving and not coming back
when they say things like that, that is what makes a poem
and actually this is exactly what words exist for
I mean for journeys, for nothingness, for disappearing
to use on the road, for eating, drinking and shelter
for going to bed, getting up, having a roof over your head
they exist to meet various kinds of needs and requirements:
humane, physical, material, moral, emotional, sexual
earthly, heavenly, animalistic, vegetative, natural, and of course human
it is a a kind of 'the poet and his partners-in-words' company
it seems like what I'm saying in my own way is this – me saying that 'poetry doesn't serve
any end, it's useless and it's futile' comes to an end with this poem as well,
and poetry as a type of comradeship shines once more on the stage of revolution!)

62

I said revolution, hey poet, this is no vaudeville, but if you really want to
you could consider it a parable, a farce, an aphorism or an instance of irony
hey revolution (also read this as 'hey poetry')
if you've arrived, knock three times, if we're not in, please leave a note,
or come by later, but do wait for us,
stay here for a few days, Istanbul is beautiful, and what is your rush anyway?
they could wait for you a little longer at wherever it is you're meant to go
and being waited for is just as good as waiting itself,
I think the poem is a journey and the journey is revolution
and I suppose right now both of them are falling asleep
I reckon this poem will end with something about how much we've loved poetry,
I had kept a line here somewhere, so it's bound to have a good ending
and besides I think a poem can be called finished when it starts falling asleep
so here follows the line I'd been saving:

– what else can death be but your life becoming sleepy?

the girls were yesterday, their breasts a stony harbour

Translated by İdil Karacadağ
from An Anthology of Love Poems (2011)

IV.

Wind

I'm out, taking the wind away with me
the house is yours
the window is yours
so is the jacket

Translated by Saliha Paker
from Such Little Things (2016)

Healing

Believing in each other, we lived far apart
just as an island stands apart from the sea,
we grew words for healing in exile
and kept them for ourselves.

Translated by Nilgün Dungan and Mel Kenne
from Such Little Things (2016)

Two Long Poems

Mutt

A house barks inside the dog
no one opens its door!

Horse

A horse dies
interred in its wind.

*Translated by Nilgün Dungan and Mel Kenne
.from* Such Little Things (2016)

Without Response

If people pose certain questions
only to themselves
they must have already got the answers
from the cross-examiner called Life
maybe that's why there is
no answer to any question

Translated by Nilgün Dungan and Mel Kenne
from Such Little Things (2016)

The Fellowship of Gullies

'Either the world or capitalism will die'
thus says the homegrown Evo Morales
the fellowship of gullies will destroy circuses too
break up the cages within and without!

Translated by Nilgün Dungan and Mel Kenne
from Such Little Things (2016)

Cemal Süreya: Translator

Cemal Süreya, a hell of a translator
translating exile into voyage
love into compassion
the world into poetry
and poetry into
– what would that be –
why fellowship of course

Translated by Nilgün Dungan and Mel Kenne
from Such Little Things (2016

Memory

We are our memories
don't forget me

We are our miseries
don't cosset me

Translated by Nilgün Dungan and Mel Kenne
from Such Little Things (2016)

Recipe for Poetry

A friend of mine's aunt is armenian
our cat was called strawberry
as to her eyes
one was profoundly green, the other deep blue
once she was white, then a smyrnian
now she's from nowhere
this recipe for poetry is from women of wisdom

Translated by Saliha Paker
from Such Little Things (2016)

The Bird of Rubaî

The bird of fancy won't perch, it flies
The bird of the heart won't stay, it flees
there's a bird in our yard
every morning and afternoon
rhymed, unrhymed or free
but like a symphony
polyphonic, variegated it trills away
I think of it as a bird of rubaî

Translated by Nilgün Dungan and Mel Kenne
from Such Little Things (2016)

What Nar Says:

Nar says:
'Come when the wind's up,
Ada said to me.'
Nar says:
'Won't the fairies break
if the glass does?'

Translated by Saliha Paker and Mel Kenne
from Such Little Things (2016)

Africa's Gift

The men of Africa
as if snapped off
the branches of a tree
flung out to the West
count for little more than leaves

Africa's green is from the men
Africa's red is from the women
Africa's yellow is from God
Africa, the loveliest colour in the world
a gift jet-black

Translated by Saliha Paker
from Such Little Things (2016)

Bough

Two mouths meeting in a kiss
seem almost to be offering each other a bough

Translated by Nilgün Dungan and Mel Kenne
from Such Little Things (2016)

The Discovery of Poetry

… It lay stark naked on a letter
then leapt over another into nought,
wanting to reach out to infinity
yet another letter withdrew in grief
refused to take part in any line
fleeing words, that was the day
I think poetry came into being,
since then so many lines
have been written so many poems,
such excess … to find that missing letter
of being

Translated by Saliha Paker
from Such Little Things (2016)

Train

Trains used to be nicer
back when we were young!

I'm not sure if I need to add these lines:
trains run a lot faster now
but our day is done.

Translated by Nilgün Dungan and Mel Kenne
from Such Little Things (2016)

Wounded

Just came out of a new poem
I'm wounded.

Translated by Nilgün Dungan and Mel Kenne
from Such Little Things (2016)

Cat

I built her a cardboard house
pasted paper over the door
stuck on a bell of her voice
poured down a shower of commas
and wrote m i l k in white letters
c'mere, kitty, come on cat of poetry

*Translated by Nilgün Dungan and Mel Kenne
from* Such Little Things (2016)

The Smell of a Poem

The tree you wrote beneath
should be clear from the poem's smell:
languid magnolia
wise olive
noble pomegranate
homebody acacia
venerable sycamore
flirtatious mulberry
amorous fig
mystical cedar…

Myrtle, Holly Oak, Locust,
Wild Olive, Mastic, Ivy,
Heather, Argan,
Arbutus, Terebinth, Laurel,
Woadwaxen, Sandalwood, Judas,
Cermes Oak, Hemlock,
Oleander, Philyrea,
Wild Pear, Soap Berry, Asparagus, Jasmine…

Bushes that smell epic,
trees that smell lyric
a poem of just this type
I've always wanted to write!

Translated by Nilgün Dungan and Mel Kenne
from Such Little Things (2016)

The Sky's Fiancée

'What if I married the sky,' you say,
no, be engaged to it instead
then you'd wear a ring of clouds
and a tiara made out of rain
we'd say you were a blue fiancée
thus arrayed until eternity
with a blue love…

Translated by Nilgün Dungan and Mel Kenne
from Such Little Things (2016)

Form

Watching the water is a form of philosophy
thinking of trees, a form of poetry
dreaming of pathways, a form of love
falling asleep, a form of solitude
boarding the train, a form of separation
writing poetry, a form of goodness
lying down to die, a form of living.

Translated by Saliha Paker
from Such Little Things (2016)

A Spirited Poem

In him was the sky spirit, flying
in him was the water spirit, flowing
in her was the earth spirit, running
so what spirit keeps you writing

whose stream are you, drifting with everyone!

Translated by Saliha Paker
from Such Little Things (2016)

Pomegranate Sea

My daughter laughs like the summer sea
looks out like an open sea
her hair The Red Sea
the Aegean scenting her words

Translated by Mel Kenne
from Such Little Things (2016)

Two Road Poems

Voyage

Adil İzci said:
for poetry I quit travelling
so what if I say in reply:
I went on a great voyage
and lost myself

Two Travelers

– I took a looooong voyage
and found myself

– I made a great voyage
and got lost

Translated by Nilgün Dungan and Mel Kenne
from Such Little Things (2016)

From *20 Love Poems*

1.

While I'm with you
I'm one person
while I'm not
I'm two alone

2.

Your being bad-natured
became a part of your nature
that's why you seem to me so blue

3.

Your flower falls short this time
I'll make it up with a smile
if your night falls a bit short as well
I'll make it up with a poem

4.

If a dream's light falls from an eye
the heart is left in the dark
(what's left is the dark heart)

5.

I'm bound to evening
from this black void
don't you unravel me

7.

What a tough nut to crack, this love
I'm broken by forty more autumns inside it
and when still green as well

*Translated by Nilgün Dungan and Mel Kenne
from* Such Little Things (2016)

V.

You Still Smell of the Sun!

As if the sun has spent the night with someone else
and not gone home until day awakes
they call this state 'the drunken ship' at times
in certain old poems and Junes of old
can June be old when the sun is yet in a state like milk
brought forth with its fire in the glass dish of morning...
A shade of Oktay Rifat would suit well here,
interpreting seals and stamps, solitary waters, old snares
and children who hunt birds with their eyes
strike wings with their voices
children, some can have rain-eyes, cloud-gazes too
their sleeps are between landscapes and sounds of summer
they smell of open-topped dreams, and warm scent of stories,
they always smell of June and a broken friendship...
Your mouth still smells of the sun, fresh sun
plucked from its branch and a little of it drizzled on the earth,
yesterday's sun is like a scrunched handkerchief, twisted
hidden in someone's lap, sniffed like a honeydew melon
in the air, the scent of a yellow sun
they all think you smell of the night, black,
but the sun is a token from your body,
and a part of your gift, still yours
perhaps you are a sun-dripped ship
all would call this drunkeness and never sober up
from this scent of the sun, don't you come to your senses
you've nothing more to hunt
the forests are closed, stars are just dust, the footpaths
have long since belonged to sky, and the hunters' caps
have the fine scent of freshly struck apples in a children's game,
love the violet mid-afternoons, caress the green declines,
feel the rose-pink daydreams, and the jacinthe-coloured lovemaking
go to her, go there mouth-to-mouth, and when her sun dawns at night
say: your mouth is more fresh than the sun

it dawns for me again each morning...
Say this three times, so the sun's milk overflows on you, too!

Translated by Caroline Stockford
from You Still Smell of the Sun! (2017)

Search Song

A bird was searching for its voice, blue
a river was searching for its water, new
a night was searching for its traveller, old
only we are not searching for each other

A stalk, tired after searching for its wind
a life, pensive after searching for its dream
a leaf, faded after searching for its autumn
oh, never has anyone searched for me like this

Would a tear search for its childhood, a wish
would suffering search for its dervish, so how
would a poem search for its lover in you
if they searched for us, in whom would we be found?

Translated by Nilgün Dungan and Mel Kenne
from You Still Smell of the Sun! (2017)

'The Bridges of Edirne'

Sunny are the bridges of Edirne.
Migrants carry the sun inside them
they carry the sun in their teeth,
shine their words with the sun
hold up their faces to the sun for a mirror,
wash their faces with the sun in the mornings
brush their teeth with the sun
and in their songs the sun never sets

To hope they trudge onward, not to despair
why be a migrant otherwise
why move elsewhere without hope
without his sun by his side
as though in the silver year of friendship
they celebrate each other
the sun and the migrant
the migrant and his sun

What you call 'sun' is the migrant's fellow-traveller
What you call 'child' is the pleasure
of gardens and fields... When the sun was out,
a long blue ray of dazzling light would fall on
the stone-paved hallway, and the child
would sit right inside that colour

'Sun' is one of two words the migrant utters
she's left behind in darkness
she can't do without the sun, says the migrant
suns cross over the stone bridge of Edirne
migrants keep crossing over the bridge
their teeth white, dreams white

Now afloat in the Maritsa, child, woman and man
their dreams dead, bodies lifeless, refugees,
never to show the sun their teeth again,
their words cold, they sink into our cruelty
drowned, drowning, to drown again…

Translated by Saliha Paker
from You Still Smell of the Sun! (2017)

Being Short

My grandmother always said: son, humans are a brief affair
and they ignore this fact, if they really knew it
they wouldn't try the roads, wouldn't build houses up to the sky
my grandmother Nazlı neither stretched a point nor pressed a claim,
her words were few, her style correct, her language a model,
footsoldiers she said are made of paltry stuff, poetry of too many words,
she was diminutive and when I lost her I realised
everything is so short, people are shorter than a tree,
shorter than evening, an apple, the sun, the snow, the rain,
even our shadows are longer than we are, in fact childhood
is shorter than its dream, look, for instance if we six kids
were to dream in shifts it would add up, maybe, to one childhood,
'This World is a Window' was an old song she used to sing
but we never got it, we're so used to the world it's hard now
to leave it, sometimes she visits my dreams, briefly, just
long enough for a smile, 'Don't spin out the poem,' she says,
'Nobody will get it and it won't lengthen your life,'
people grow with their mistakes, I used to think that love was long,
then it came to me – but when! – that it's shorter than its four letters,
sometimes it vanishes as you write, sometimes it takes a while
to redeem it from the forest within, love is short, poetry long,
if a tree gets lost in a forest, the forest is still a forest,
right, but what if a letter disappears from 'human,'
how many did we have to begin with?

Translated by Clifford Endres and Selhan Savcıgil-Endres
from You Still Smell of the Sun! (2017)

Fresh Like the Old Summers

for my İdil

Why is loving you forever fresh in me like the old summers
as something remembered more and more often
perhaps like recollecting loving too is as pleasurable,
healing and necessary, shall we say, as lining up
little bits of rock in a row, stacking them one on top of the other,
if so, then let this ritual be a gesture from our astrological signs
to us both, while our little bits of rock are of different hues
so we can aim at each other's heart yet spare each other the hurt.
Since only you can save me from poetry and only you
can throw me back into poetry once more – write,
and say we were born for each other right on a summer's day
hence, I only feel like summer towards you, nothing else, yet summer
never seems to pass in you, a love-timer that has stopped,
always running slow, slowing down for us
it mustn't run faster, summer mustn't outrun us
if we were to race ahead of it, where would we go
let us forget, forget, it'll wear out if we don't
remembering is like the first time ever, everything
so let us remember, for remembering is forever
fresh like the old summers, always good like loving you…

Translated by Saliha Paker
from You Still Smell of the Sun! (2017)

Rainy Garden

Is it raining in your garden?
– No, the rain's in my eyes…
Will you allow my poems in
as visitors then?

My words send kisses
in greeting to your garden…

Translated by Nilgün Dungan and Mel Kenne
unpublished poem (2019)

Saturday

I've loved you since Saturday
the world was created on a Saturday, you know
I can't say if it's that old or that new
my Saturday love of you

Translated by Nilgün Dungan and Mel Kenne
unpublished poem (2019)

Green Duck

…and just as I'd chosen that green dress for you
your eyes came to mind, I looked,
but your eyes were not green enough for this poem
besides I'd never seen you cry,
and it was pointless
seeking the traces of tears in the eyes
of one whose words are nothing but lies…
the month was June supposedly, April and September
stumbled arm in arm like a couple of drunks
passing our road, their eyes full of rain
then I knew why songs in a downpour sound stammered
Ask the apple about love, don't ask me, look at the rain
I've no room left within, place the pain outside of me!
Had I a shirt of green I'd have joined in all your songs
I have no shirt of green and that child, he isn't me
that child is at the age of rhymes, I can't rain grief on him
someone else wanders your body, and the pain of it crushes my soul
whosoever opens his shirt to you, let him write you his poetry
on flesh, tattoos will fade, but on the soul they stay the same
I've been tattooed by the drumming rain
it's best not to eat the greenest plums, don't moan to me when your belly aches
and if you catch a cold let someone else fetch you a green scarf
but remember no one sings the folk song as profoundly as me
and I dived in the lakes like a green, green duck
have I never sung it you, then that means I've never seen
not one drop of tears, bitter rain, on your lashes
take offence, ignore me then, don't ever come past our street again!

Translated by Caroline Stockford
from You Still Smell of the Sun! (2017)

Once a Child

This childhood is something like the sky, not going anywhere
a line that's half one's childhood,
that can only be spoken by one who's half-child
maybe poetry writing's more or less like this
half of it flying the kite of words
half knotting new ones onto the kite's tail
new…but what, new words only?
new words, yes, like new marbles, sparkly
new clouds so where they go doesn't matter
with them anywhere becomes a sky an evernew sky
but, like childhood they always linger on in ourplace inside us
don't sell ourplace short, it's not much but it's ours
poetry after all, isn't a big deal, could any poem
be more lovely than childhood, no, how do I know this, again
from poetry, again from childhood, again from myself
I wish I knew, trying to be half a child myself
write poetry, fall in love, make kids, travel the world,
all, you see, to catch up with childhood
that hasn't really gone anywhere
then say to yourself slow down, hold on a minute
you're an old townie once a child, this sky
this childhood, where else can they be found? I hear, I stop,
for you can only catch up with childhood if you stay put
so you do the growing up, I'm staying right here!

Translated by Arzu Eker Roditakis and Mel Kenne
from You Still Smell of the Sun! (2017)

The Heavenly Carousel

I saw my father in heaven
he was going around on a carousel
hopping off one horse onto another
clearly not ready to leave childhood

one of those sleepless kids, my dad
got halfway through middle school
before leaving it to enrol in life
and then in the poetry of Ece Ayhan

in his youth his hair had concealed
the gentleness of his eyes
but when that hill was barren of hair
all the kindness in his eyes broke out

an only child, yet a father to so many
like Pappa Can, so childlike himself,
when most skilful a novice, my father
of us all the one most a child

I never saw his helpers but in my mind still
see them at work, repairing tac-a-tac-a-tac
first, as children, the grown-ups' cars
then, when grown, their childhood selves

What do I know about heaven?
It wasn't heaven I saw but my dad
a man who'd turned this life into paradise
could only turn that side into paradise too!

Translated by İdil Karacadağ and Mel Kenne
from You Still Smell of the Sun! (2017)

The Neighbouring Island

In the backrooms of their homes some kids miss the sea
aiming to become a sea when they grow up, they dream in blue
can a provincial place be imagined blue where no one can stray too far from one
    another
imagined or not, what do I care about the sea
when Emel's green eyes are enough to turn even a good boy into a poet!
Kids' eyes are like islands that wink at each other as if
they're two loving beacons, one asleep while the other's awake.
We had no island but our neighbours were many
I thought of my mother as an immigrant among them
we had no sea either since brotherliness was thick as sand
we had Rose, new mother, old 'bigsister',
grandma had raged at me and my brother Kemal as we gaped,
'Well, I never! She's not your bigsister, Rose is your mum!'
We'd gone red even in the shade, and Rose looked more abashed than us
'bigsister', my brother and me, we could never have healed without our courtyard,
we'd just arrived from the neighbouring island and moved into its bountiful shade
migrant freckles on my mum's face, left over from afternoon chats with neighbours
in my mind Emel, my first love, a neighbourly memory from the island
they say poetry's written when you're grown up and your first love's forgotten
if poetry is written in order to forget, then I'm out, so is this poem,
I want my mum to be my bigsister again and the island to replace the immigrant
    settlement
then I won't ever grow up, or become a sea, rather than forgetting my first love
I won't write poetry but be the neighbour's kid instead, if only
to keep that memory inside me swinging back and forth!

Translated by Saliha Paker
from You Still Smell of the Sun! (2017)

Your Meadows

is your heart pomegranate-coloured for nothing?
is your soul such a deep blue for nothing?
is your dream a lush green for nothing?
is your name brimful of laughter for nothing?

Your meadows' yield is poetry!

*Translated by Nilgün Dungan and Mel Kenne
from* Idyllics (2019)

Poem of Birds

Is there a people older than the birds
A poem more lofty than they
A sea bluer than birds
A green that precedes them
Are there people beyond the birds?

If the sky does not belong to birds
then where is poetry's home?

Is there a folk more closely
tied to their tradition than birds?
As freedom is the oldest custom
and birds bound to it by their wings

Birds are as plenty as nothing
as good as a little
new as a smile
absent as flight

Poetry tells us, birds
came first to the world
oh, the world of birdcoming
birds heighten its vault
birds exalt the sky

Translated by Caroline Stockford
from You Still Smell of the Sun! (2017)

Pomegranate Garden

Between your words you fit in a breathing spell
into your silence you fit the long sunny summers
into your memories the poetry of your twin-plaited childhood
and into your gaze two delicately clinking glasses getting acquainted
leaving the glass of this evening unbroken you fit soul into soul
into your haste you fit a winter sea's old ferry
you fit in crossing the water always blue
and into your heart's garden
of a thousandfold loving of a pomegranate
you fit the pomegranate garden

Translated by Saliha Paker and Mel Kenne
from Idyllics (2019)

VI.

Abdal Going Slowly on His Way

He's my sovereign and comrade, my ongoingness
lifeless walls he rides driving them on and on
in a pigeon's habit he flies, in a gazelle's races onward
in a lion's company has crossed this town often
it's Abdal who now slowly spreads
Hacı Bektaş Velî's paths
with the poems of his ongoingness:

'If the wall moved would the mountain stay still
if the mountain moved would the wood stay still
why is wood crafted from the spirit-tree
of life, I'm the shadow, I think
of my childhood, that tree is mine
from a mother I seem to have grown a body,
and from woodwork to poetry I've come, a spirit,
not from a word or feeling but from a courtyard,
like a shadow I'd have to say I've come

One born bears life, the tree bears life, and the courtyard
because all things start out female
feelings, images, poems, words
the leaf's female, water's female, the apple's female
sleep's female, while dreams, I'd say, are angels,
I can't vouch for the traveller, but the journey's female
let's go to the provinces to get back in touch
their interiors, their afternoons, their homes, their rivers
their abandonment are all female, like their solitude and waste lands
because mother who's a journey is female too...

It's the absence of sea, they say, from this privation
the provinces hold their secret femaleness within,
such solitude could've grown from this lack
if, as with a mother city, time's 'old' version
hadn't passed by subtly with a river's experience,

what's transitory we don't call new but to what gently
holds onto the old we say you're new, you're good,
this is why if the lack of sea is privation,
if the poet's humility is good, so will the city have mercy
we also call the city old to keep it in the courtyard
that crafted wood may remain within the city's mercy
the weary, the defeated, the captive, the passions,
hotels, inns, coffeehouses, rains,
old script, old poetry, old city are all
in that yard, they're all there for that yard, what's made of wood is that yard
as its paving stones washed in mercy are set in woodwork too.

This town is female, as is that city, this poem
mother is female, our sea is there, in the old
if our mother's there too, she must be in the poetry
we've become from her shadow a tree was growing
tall in the shade of a house, its front taller
grown with the woodwork, I haven't forgotten
you were spirit and we in your courtyard were walnut, fig, mulberry
and young trees in that yard, you were my friends, you're still there
those there never abandon their spirit, their spirit moves
nowhere without them I took my shadow with me when leaving
my childhood not spirit nor tree nor yard nor woodwork
which is why I'm my own shadow too
from her meagre childhood I took away my mother's shadow as well
becoming a shadow for poetry too this is why like an apparition
sometimes I pass through our houses, our cities, our pigeons,
our cranes, our trains, and our less poetic
street dogs, street cats, street children,
our street men, street women this is why we love them all
and send our greetings to them as a journey
because we too are expected by a mother to return, we're loved and missed,
for no poetry or journey would we trade that,
because our mother never sent us off to poetry or in fact anywhere
in fact there's no journey from somewhere to someplace else
when everything's in its place, where to the journey,

who leaves, who stays behind?
what changes place is only a shadow perhaps we're all
curious to know what passes through it, and imagine ourselves journeying
maybe what's real is our shadow if so to what do we belong
and why are we, everyone's on the way what a long way this is
no one to arrive at their destination nor to return
if we were pilgrims not travellers long ago we would've
set off on a journey from a sojourn now done in this world
or is it that we're taking a rest not knowing why we left
how do we get back where was our route still an ocean farther away
leaving is sometimes like this, passing through staying, staying put

This may be the most lyrical journey of all showing that poetry's on track
our poetry is female too, so are our words and our commas
because home is female, mother is female and woodwork is transitory
meaning on loan, not everlasting, nor should it be
all we have has come to this courtyard to be forgotten
to pass on, the poetry stays, the journey passes and so
get on, stay put, set out, move along, go, leave, pass by, move on
if one name of all that we love is woodwork the other's Abdal
in the slow mode of music a wondrous, gentle Abdal
a passing feeling that almost takes its own place
an absence that never invites a presence, this Abdal slow

In Senegal a poor man seeking his spirit in the baobab tree
how shouldn't he be thought poor with his spirit enriched by leaves
and just as they've found a leaf sister for their spirit
who appears to travel on the body of that tree
so Abdal slowly fulfils his period of ordeal in the assembly of forty
oh salt oh bread oh water oh olive oh wine oh pomegranate oh they
know yet forget how their convent was knit together with the patience of woodwork
to carry this mystery they keep travelling through the world, keep travelling
otherwise the secret will fall from their shoulders as will the spirit…'

What I ask now is Abdal's slow question oh where are you?
They who pass by walk on, they who remain stop, mother woodwork
gives birth to spirit, evening falls on the courtyard poetry sets
so I won't go out to hunt for deer
between two eyebrows a mother has her seat
this poem doesn't end here it's only complete

Translated by Saliha Paker and Mel Kenne
from You Still Smell of the Sun! (2017)

Notes on Poems

We're Lonely Brother Cemal:

Cemal Süreya (1931-1990) was a leading poet of the Turkish Second New Movement. His book, *Pigeonwoman / Üvercinka,* was translated by Donny Smith and Abbas Karakaya. Kars is a province in the north-east of Turkey, bordering Russia.

Borrowed Like Sorrow:

'*...nothing / asked of all those who stay silent*': from the poem 'İki Başına Yürümek' (To Walk Two-In-One) by Behçet Necatigil (1916-1979), one of the foremost Turkish poets of the 20th century. Many English translations of his poetry can be found in *Turkish Poetry Today 2016.*

'There's no train in the poem / So why all this grief?': inspired by lines from Cemal Süreya's 'Kısa Türkiye Tarihi V'(Short History of Turkey).

Ece Ayhan (1931-2002), like Cemal Süreya, was a major poet of the Turkish Second New Movement.' His book, *A Blind Cat Black and Orthodoxies,* was translated by Murat Nemet-Nejat.

'Hasan's eyes': Haydar's father's eyes.

'Selahattin's eyes': Seyhan's father's eyes.

Seyhan Erözçelik (1962-2011) was a leading poet of the 1980s. His book, *Rosestrikes and Coffee Grinds,* was translated by Murat Nemet-Nejat.

'Old script' refers to Turkish in Arabic script, which was abolished in 1927, four years after the declaration of the Turkish Republic.

Gazel Of Secrets:

The *gazel* (ghazal) is a classical Turkish verse form of Persian origin, which is devoted to love, ranging from worldly to mystical.

Gazel of Orphans:

Hrant Dink (1954-2007), an Armenian-Turkish journalist who founded and became chief editor of the newspaper *Agos*, was assassinated in front of his office in Istanbul on January 19, 2007.

Cem, an annual ritual assembly of the Alevî-Bektaşî.

Semah is a ritual dance of the Alevî-Bektaşî tradition, participated in by both women and men.

Inner *Nefes*:

Nefes denotes a narrative verse form that is sung in Alevî-Bektaşî rituals.

Write a Letter:

Sheikh Galip (1757–1799), the foremost Ottoman poet of the 18th century, is famous for his mystical narrative *Beauty and Love*, translated by Victoria Holbrook.

Erzurum is a province in north-east Turkey.

Tahtakuşlar is a village near Mt. Ida in the North Aegean region of Turkey, known for its shamanic origins and traditions.

Aşık Mahzunî Şerif (1939-2002) and Ali Ekber Çicek (1935-2006), both of Alevî-Bektaşî origin, were folk singers renowned throughout Turkey.

The Grand Arcade is located in central Ankara, the capital city of Turkey.

Tanju Okan: (1938-1996) was a pop-singer and film star with lifelong popularity.

The Garden of Departed Cats is a famous work of fiction written by novelist and essayist Bilge Karasu (1930-1995). It was translated into English by Aron Aji.

The Kid with the Green Shirt:

Turgut Uyar (1927-1985) was one of the most renowned poets of the Second New Movement.

I Could Never Be An Evening!:

'*You my offbeat, oddball darling*
How quickly evening has descended unnoticed': from 'Harp Kaldırımında Aşk' (Love on the Pavement of War) by Atilla İlhan (1925-2005), one of the most popular poets of his time, who was also a novelist and critic.

Translation:

The terms 'old body…new language' refer to the old corpora of Ottoman classical poetry in Arabic script and to new Turkish, advanced after the language 'purification' reform to eliminate words derived from Arabic and Persian.

On Things That Are Falling Asleep:

Cemal Süreya (noted previously) was a leading poet of the Second New movement.

Kızılbaş (*Quizilbash*) means 'red head' and was once used as a byword for Kurds. It has now fallen into disrepute.

The lines '*with the joy / of there being no sleep beneath anybody's eyelids*' are a modification by Haydar Ergülen of a Turkish translation of an epitaphic poem by Rainer Maria Rilke that reads in John J. L. Mood's English translation as 'Rose, oh pure contradiction, desire, / To be no one's sleep under so many / Lids.'

Odunpazarı, Yoğurtçu Park, Kadıköy, etc., refer to neighbourhoods and districts in Eskişehir, Istanbul and Ankara.

Süha Tuğtepe, (1956-2009) was a Turkish a poet.

Dirty August is a poetry collection by Edip Cansever (1928-1986), another well known poet of the Second New movement. It was translated into English by Richard and Julia Clare Tillinghast.

You Still Smell of the Sun!:

Oktay Rifat (1914-1988) was a revered poet of the *Garip* (Strange) Movement of the 1940s and 1950s. 'Interpreting seals and stamps' refers to his collection, *Eski Mühürler* (Old Seals and Stamps). A selection of his poetry, *Voices of Memory*, was translated by Ruth Christie and Richard McKane.

'The Bridges of Edirne':

This poem is a tribute to *Parasız Yatılı* (Free Boarding School) by Füruzan (1932-), a leading short fiction writer of the 1970s and 1980s, who was herself an immigrant from the Balkans. Some lines are excerpted from her story of the same title.

Once a Child:

The line quoted at the beginning of this poem is from the poem 'Manastırlı Hilmi Bey'e İkinci Mektup' (Second Letter to Hilmi Bey of Manastır) by Edip Cansever.

The Heavenly Carousel:

Ece Ayhan (noted previously) was a leading poet of the Second New movement.

Pappa Can (for *Can Baba*) was an affectionate nickname for poet Can Yücel (1926-1999), renowned for his witty and satirical poems. A selection of his poetry was translated into English by Feyyaz Kayacan Fergar.

Cemal Süreya: Translator:

Cemal Süreya (noted previously) was a leading poet of the Second New Movement.

What Nar Says:

Haydar Ergülen's daughter's name is Nar. Ada is the name of another girl.

Voyage:

Adil İzci (1954-) is a Turkish poet and essayist.

Abdal Going Slowly on His Way:

'we call the city old to keep it in the courtyard...' and 'old script, old poetry, old city...' all refer to Eskişehir (meaning old town/city) where Ergülen spent his childhood.

Translator Biographies

Arzu Akbatur holds a PhD degree in Translation Studies from Boğaziçi University, with her dissertation entitled 'Writing / Translating in / to English: the "Ambivalent" Case of Elif Shafak' (2011). She received her BA and MA degrees in English Language and Literature from Boğaziçi and Yeditepe Universities, respectively. She has taught courses on translation at several universities in Turkey. Her main research interests include literary translation, translation theories, Turkish literature in English translation, and translation and representation.

Gökçenur Ç. was born in Istanbul in 1971 and still lives there. Seven books of his poetry have been published, and he has translated books by such contemporary poets as Wallace Stevens, Paul Auster, and Ursula K. Le Guin. He has participated in and organised poetry translation workshops and festivals in many countries, while his own poems have been translated into twenty-five languages and published in magazines and anthologies in Italy, Bulgaria, Romania, and Serbia. He founded and co-directs the international translation organisation Word Express and is a member of the Cunda International Workshop for Translators of Turkish Literature, which he has attended as a visiting writer as well. He is also an editor of the Turkish literature magazine *Çevrimdışı İstanbul* (Offline İstanbul) and a member of the editorial board of the Macedonian-based international literary magazine *Blesok*.

Nilgün Dungan is a lecturer and a translator based in Izmir, Turkey. She studied English Language and Literature at Ege University and received a master's degree in Administrative Management from Bowie State University, in Maryland. She taught English and Business classes at Minot State University, in North Dakota. Her translation into English of *Remembering Atatürk* won an Honourable Mention in the Best Publishing House translation competition. Currently she is pursuing her PhD in Translation Studies at Boğaziçi University and teaching in the Department of English Translation and Interpretation at Izmir University of Economics. She has been a participant of the Cunda Workshop of Translators of Turkish Literature since 2007 as a translator into English of Turkish fiction and poetry. Her translations of articles and short stories have been published in journals and magazines, and she translated Müge İplikçi's novel *Mount Qaf* (Milet 2013).

Clifford Endres has taught at the University of Texas at Austin and at Ege, Boğaziçi, Başkent, and Kadir Has universities in Turkey. He is the author of *Joannes Secundus: The Latin Love Elegy in the Renaissance* (1981) and *Austin City Limits* (1987). His Turkish translations, in collaboration notably with Selhan Savcıgil-Endres and Saliha Paker, have appeared in *Absinthe, Agenda, Edinburgh Review, Massachusetts Review, Quarterly West*, and *Seneca Review* among others. His most recent publication is *Edouard Roditi ve İstanbul Avangardı* (Kırmızı Kedi Yayınevi, 2018). First published as 'Edouard Roditi and the Istanbul Avant-Garde' in *Texas Studies in Language and Literature,* 54 (2012), it was translated into Turkish by Selhan Savcıgil-Endres.

Şehnaz Tahir Gürçağlar is professor of translation studies and teaches in the graduate programmes at Glendon College (York University) and Boğaziçi University (Istanbul). Her main fields of interest are translation history, ideology and translation and periodical studies. She is the author of *Politics and Poetics of Translation in Turkey* (Rodopi, 2008) and co-editor of *Tradition, Tension and Translation in Turkey* (Benjamins, 2015) and *Perspectives on Retranslation: Ideology, Paratexts, Methods* (Routledge, 2018). Her poetry translations have been published in *Aeolian Visions / Versions* (2013) and *Blue Lyra Review* (2013). She served on the steering committee of Cunda International Workshop for Translators of Turkish Literature.

İdil Karacadağ was born in Istanbul in 1991. She acquired her BA in Literature at Kadir Has University and spent a year at Bath Spa University as an exchange student. She participated in the Cunda International Workshop for Translators of Turkish Literature in 2010, 2013, 2014, and 2015. She has translated various contemporary Turkish poets into English, and co-translated, with Mel Kenne, two novels and a novella by Zülfü Livaneli. Her translations have been published in *Turkish Poetry Today* and in the collection of Cunda translations, *Aeolian Visions / Versions: Modern Classics and New Writing from Turkey, from the Cunda International Workshop for Translators of Turkish Literature, 2006-2012* (Milet Publishing 2013).

Elizabeth Pallitto holds a master's in Creative Writing and and a PhD in Literature from NYU and CUNY respectively. Having taught in New York and Istanbul, she now leads creative writing workshops at Rutgers and Highland Park, NJ. She is the editor of *Leaves of Autumn* (Ashford & Rome: Epos, 2015), which grew out of her 'WiLL' (Writers in League with Libraries) workshop. This Library-based group, in its fourth year, is still going strong. In addition to working with Turkish poetry, Pallitto translates from French and Italian. She is the editor and translator of the Renaissance Italian poems in *Sweet Fire: Tullia d'Aragona's Poetry of Dialogue* (Braziller, 2007).

Arzu Eker Roditakis has a BA in Communication Studies from Istanbul University and an MA degree in Translation Studies from Boğaziçi University, where she also began her doctoral studies and gave courses on translation theory, practice, and criticism. Her MA thesis, titled *Publishing Translations in the Social Sciences since the 1980s: An Alternative View of Culture Planning in Turkey,* was published in 2010 by Lambert Academic Publishing. She has also taught academic English at Boğaziçi and Yeditepe Universities. Currently she resides in Greece, where she completed her PhD degree in Translation Studies at Aristotle University of Thessaloniki with a dissertation analysing the English translations of Orhan Pamuk's novels. She has also given courses at Aristotle University and the American College of Thessaloniki. She presently divides her time between independent research, translation, and teaching English online.

Selhan Savcıgil-Endres has taught at Hacettepe, Başkent, and Kadir Has universities and written on Turkish and American authors such as Orhan Pamuk, Toni Morrison, and Paul Auster. Her translations of poetry and drama by Enis Batur, Güven Turan, Gülten Akın, Haldun Taner and many others have appeared in, among other publications, *An Anthology of Modern Turkish Drama, Eda: An Anthology of Contemporary Turkish Poetry, New European Poets, The Edinburgh Review, The Massachusetts Review, Near East Review, Quarterly West, Seneca Review,* and *Talisman.* She translated, with Clifford Endres, two novels by Selçuk Altun: *Many and Many a Year Ago* (2009) and *The Sultan of Byzantium* (2012). She also translated *Edouard Roditi ve İstanbul Avangardı* (Istanbul: Kırmızı Kedi Yayınevi, 2018).

İpek Seyalıoğlu teaches at Boğaziçi University in Istanbul. She holds a master's degree in graphic novels from Paris VIII St.Denis-Vincennes and a master's in literary translation from Boğaziçi University. Her award-winning play, *Copper Shield,* and many of her poems, short stories, and translations have been published in literary journals in Turkey and abroad. She translated Mel Kenne's poetry collection *The View from Galata* and contributed to the anthology *A Hundred Streets of Istanbul from 101*

Writers. She studied acting and art with Şahika Tekand in Studio Players, in Istanbul, and has attended a number of workshops abroad, including the Biomechanics of Meyerhold, in Italy, with Genadi Bogdanov, Liquid Action at the Grotowski Institute, with Matej Matejka, and the Method of Dionysos at Attis Theatre, with Theodoros Terzopoulos. She has participated in various plays and short films and is currently writing her own play and collaborating with other groups as a performer, writer, and director.

Acknowledgements

The following translations of poems and talks by Haydar Ergülen included in this book, or slightly different versions of them, have appeared previously in the following publications:

Nar: '96: A Selection: 'Love's Inflection in Turkish' and 'Cardboard Suitcase'.

Aeolian Visions / Versions: Modern Classics and New Writing from Turkey: 'The Poet's Share of Words: Excerpt from a Talk by Haydar Ergülen', 'Letter to God', 'We're Lonely, Brother Cemal', 'Carry Us Across', 'Kuzguncuk Hotel', 'Lost Brother', and 'Ghazal of Idylls'.

Turkish Poetry Today 2015: 'Love Is Small', 'And She Says', '*Nefes* of Inner Breath', '*Nefes* of the Quiet Between Us', 'The Green Duck', and 'On Things That Are Falling Asleep'.

Parthian Fiction

Hummingbird
Tristan Hughes
ISBN 978-1-91-090190-8
£8.99 ● Paperback

Winner of Edward Standford Award

Ironopolis
Glen James Brown
ISBN 978-1-91-268109-9
£8.99 ● Paperback

'A triumph'
– The Guardian

Pigeon
Alys Conran
ISBN 978-1-91-090123-6
£8.99 ● Paperback

Winner of Wales Book of the Year

Winner of Rhys Davies Award

The Long Dry
(Granta edition)
Cynan Jones
ISBN 978-1-78-378040-2
£8.99 ● Paperback

'A convincing glimpse of life,
in all its beauty and its sadness.'
– Big Issue

PARTHIAN

CARNIVALE

2 0 1 9 / 2 1

La Blanche
Maï-Do Hamisultane
Translated by Suzy Ceulan Hughes
ISBN 978-1-91-268123-5
£8.99 • Paperback

The Night Circus
and Other Stories
Uršuľa Kovalyk
Translated by Julia and
Peter Sherwood
ISBN 978-1-91-268104-4
£8.99 • Paperback

Fiction in Translation

The Book of Katerina
Auguste Corteau
Translated by Claire Papamichael
ISBN 978-1-91-268126-6
£8.99 • Paperback

TRANSLATED BY CLAIRE PAPAMICHAEL

The Book of Katerina
Auguste Corteau

'Filled with magical words, therapeutic, artistic... and playful. Playful about the women who strain, about the women who suffer...'
MIREN IBARLUZEA, *BIZKAIE*

A Glass Eye
Miren Agur Meabe

A Glass Eye
Miren Agur Meabe
Translated by Amaia Gabantxo
ISBN 978-1-91-210954-8
£8.99 • Paperback

Her Mother's Hands
Karmele Jaio
Translated by Kristin Addis
ISBN 978-1-91-210955-5
£8.99 • Paperback

WINNER
ENGLISH PEN
AWARD

WINNER
Euskadi Plata Prize

WINNER
Zazpi Kale Prize

Seventh Igartza Prize

'Jaio is undoubtedly a very skilful narrator'
IÑIGO ROQUE, GARA

Her Mother's Hands
Karmele Jaio

PARTHIAN
CARNIVALE
2 0 1 9 / 2 1